SUPERCLUBS

UNOFFICIAL

SOCCER YEARBOOK 98/99

FOR SUPPORTERS OF

NOTTS COUNTY

First published in Great Britain in 1998 by
Dempsey Parr
13 Whiteladies Road
Clifton
Bristol BS8 1PB

ISBN: 1840841230

Produced for Dempsey Parr by
Prima Creative Services

Editorial director Roger Kean
Managing editor Tim Smith (Content E.D.B.)
Contributing authors
Steve Bradley
Jim Drewett (Deadline Features)
Steve Farragher
Sam Johnstone
Alex Leith (Deadline Features)
Rex Nash
Russell Smith
Tim Smith

Cover background and illustrations by Oliver Frey

Design and repro by Prima Creative Services

Printed and bound in Italy by L.E.G.O., Vicenza

Picture Acknowledgements
The publisher would like to thank the staff of Allsport and Action Images for their unstinting help and all the other libraries, newspapers and photographers who have made this edition possible. All pictures are credited alongside the photograph.

ACTION IMAGES

SUPERCLUBS
UNOFFICIAL SOCCER YEARBOOK 98/99
FOR SUPPORTERS OF

NOTTS COUNTY

CONTENTS

STATISTICS

The world's oldest surviving football club, Notts County are also the only team to have entered the FA Cup every year since 1877. The Magpies even won the competition once, back in 1894, but have only occasionally threatened to win some serious silverware since. But that was then... storming Division Three last season has inspired the kind of confidence that can't be manufactured. 1998-99 will surely see the momentum maintained and Division One can only be a matter of 'keep on keeping on' for the Meadow Lane Marauders.

Date Formed: 1864
Date Entered Football League: 1888

Former Names:	Notts Football Club
Official Nickname:	The Magpies
Other Nicknames:	County

Sam Allardyce: the sweet taste of success

Magpies joy as Gary Jones scores the first in a handsome defeat of Barnet, 7/3/98. This kind of effort should terrorise Division Two opponents

MANAGERS SINCE JOINED LEAGUE:

Edwin Browne	(1883–93)	Arthur Stollery	(1946–49)	Howard Wilkinson	(1982–83)
Tom Featherstone	(1893)	Eric Houghton	(1949–53)	Larry Lloyd	(1983–84)
Tom Harris	(1893–1913)	George Poyser	(1953–57)	Richie Barker	(1984–85)
Albert Fisher	(1913–27)	Tommy Lawton	(1957–58)	Jimmy Sirrel	(1985–87)
Horace Henshall	(1927–34)	Frank Hill	(1958–61)	John Barnwell	(1987–88)
Charlie Jones	(1934–35)	Tim Coleman	(1961–63)	Neil Warnock	(1989–93)
David Pratt	(1935)	Eddie Lowe	(1963–65)	Mick Walker	(1993–94)
Percy Smith	(1935–36)	Tim Coleman	(1965–66)	Russell Slade	(1994–95)
Jimmy McMullan	(1936–37)	Jack Burkitt	(1966–67)	Howard Kendall	(1995)
Harry Parkes	(1938–39)	Billy Gray	(1967–68)	Colin Murphy	(1995)
Tony Towers	(1939–42)	Jimmy Sirrel	(1968–75)	Steve Thompson	(1996)
Frank Womack	(1942–43)	Ron Fenton	(1975–77)	Sam Allardyce	(1997–)
Major F. Buckley	(1944–46)	Jimmy Sirrel	(1978–82)		

CLUB HONOURS

FA Cup Winners 1894 (March 31st, Goodison Park)
Notts County v Bolton Wanderers 4–1
Scorers: Logan (3), Watson

FA Cup Runners Up 1891 (March 21st, Kennington Oval)
Blackburn Rovers v Notts County 3–1; Scorer: Oswald

Anglo-Italian Cup Winners 1995 (March 19th, Wembley)
Notts County v Ascoli 2–1; Scorers: Agana, White

Anglo-Italian Cup Runners–Up 1994 (March 20th, Wembley)
Brescia v Notts County 1–0

Division Two Champions
1897, 1914, 1923

Division Two Runners–Up
1895, 1981

Division Two Play-off winners
1991

Division Three (South) Champions
1931, 1950

Division Three (South) Runners–Up
1937

Division Three Runners–Up
1973

Division Three Play-off winners
1990

Division Four Champions
1971

Division Four Runners–Up
1960

Chairman: DC Pavis
Club Sponsors: SAPA (Aluminium Extrusions)

Record Attendance: 47,310 against York City, FA Cup 6th Round, March 12th 1955

Action Images

The picture speaks louder than words – watch out Div Two!

Stadiums: 1862–64 The Park
1864–77 The Meadows
1877–80 Beeston Cricket Ground
1880–81 Trent Bridge
1881–83 Castle Cricket Ground
1883–1910 Trent Bridge
1910– Meadow Lane

Address: County Ground, Meadow Lane, Nottingham NG2 3HJ

Capacity: 20,300

Stands: Jimmy Sirrel Stand, Derek Pavis Stand, Family Stand, Kop Stand, (Family Enclosure: Family Stand)

Prices: Adults £11, £13, £15
Senior Citizens £6, £9, £10; Children £5, £7, £7.50

Season ticket prices: Adults £187–£275
Senior Citizens £115.50–£192.50
Children £104.50–£165; Family Magpie Club £20 (under-12), £50 (under-16)

Parking facilities: Club car park, Meadow Lane

PITCH DIMENSIONS

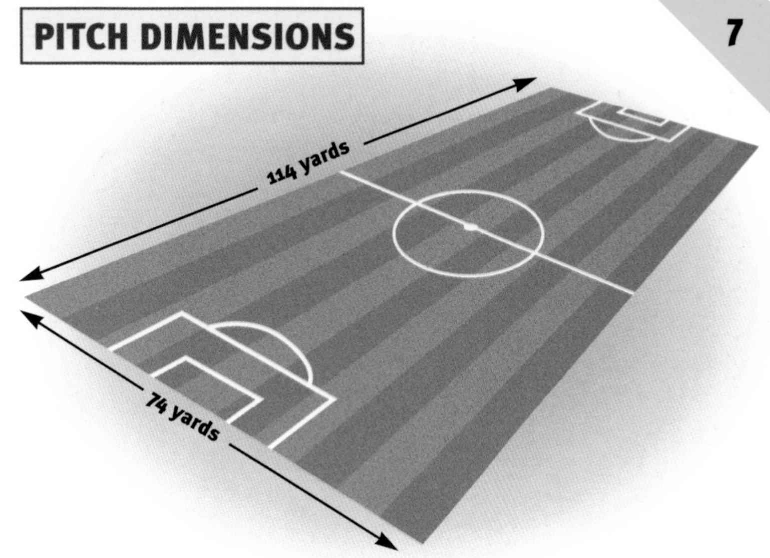

Preferred team formation: 4–4–2
Biggest rivals: Nottingham Forest

Programme: Notts County Programme
Programme Editor: Terry Bowles
Programme Price: £1.30
Bus routes to stadium: A60, Nottingham train station and buses 1, 6, 9, 10, 12, 61, 61A, 62, 63, 68, 70, 85, 90, 95

BEST PUB

The World Renowned Trent Bridge Inn, 2 Radcliffe Road

ACTION IMAGES

Sean Farrell – 15 league goals last season

FANZINES

The Pie 51 Ashworth Avenue, Ruddington, Nottingham NG11 6GD

Flicking 'N' Kicking 7 Loughborough Road, Burton on the Wolds, Loughborough LE12 4AF

No More Pie in the Sky 39 Dunvegan Drive, Rise Park. Nottingham, NG5 5DX

The Better Half, 352 Hillmorton Road, Rugby CV22 5EY

CONTACT NUMBERS

(Tel Code 0115)

- Main number 952 9000
- Fax 955 3994
- Ticket Office 955 7210
- Matchday info 952 9000
- Commercial dept 952 9000
- Supporters Club 955 7255
- Club shop 952 9000
- Clubcall 888684

LEADING PLAYERS

A club needs stars, but it's all the players who make up a team, and here are some Magpies who will be storming up through Division Two during 1998-99, including (above) March newcomer Andrew Hughes, the 20-year-old bright prospect who signed from Oldham Athletic for £150,000

ACTION IMAGES

1997/98 SEASON TOP 10 GOALSCORERS

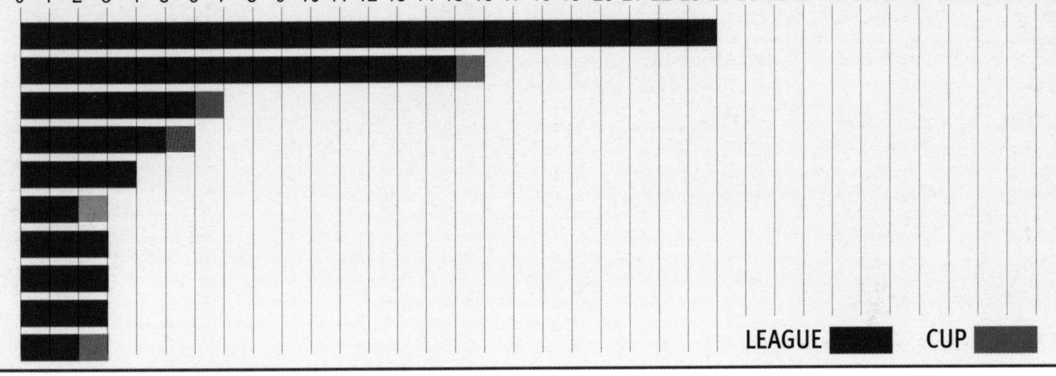

MOST LEAGUE APPEARANCES

PLAYER		APPEARANCES	SUBSTITUTE	GOALS
1	Steve Finnan	41	3	5
2	Gary Jones	43	1	24
3	Darren Ward	44	0	0
4	Phil Robinson	30	10	3
5	Gary Strodder	37	2	4
6	Ian Baraclough	36	2	6
7	Ian Hendon	38	0	0
8	Dennis Pearce	37	1	1
9	Sean Farrell	32	3	15
10	Matthew Redmile	32	2	3
11	Ian Richardson	25	5	1
12	Shaun Derry	27	1	2
13	Mark Robson	26	2	3
14	Gary Martindale	5	17	1
15	Craig Dudley	5	12	2
16	Andrew Hughes	12	3	2
17	Justin Jackson	4	11	1
18	Alex Dyer	10	0	0
19	Shaun Cunnington	3	6	0
20	Tony Lormor	2	5	0

PLAYER STATISTICS

Record transfer fee paid:
Tony Agana – £625,000 from Sheffield Utd (November 1991)

Record transfer fee received:
Craig Short – £2,500,000 from Derby County (September 1992)

Oldest player: Albert Iremonger, 41 years and 320 days against Huddersfield, May 1st 1926

Youngest player: Tony Bircumshaw, 16 years and 54 days against Brentford, April 3rd 1961

International captains:
Martin O'Neill (Northern Ireland)

Most capped player:
Kevin Wilson (15) Northern Ireland (1992–93)

SQUAD

MICHAEL POLITT

DOB: 29/2/72
Position: Goalkeeper
Usual shirt number: 1
Joined club: November 1995 from Darlington
League Games played: 10
League Goals scored: 0
International caps: 0
League Debut: 10/12/96 v Scarborough (A), Auto Windscreens Shield 1st round

DARREN WARD

DOB: 11/5/74
Position: Goalkeeper
Usual shirt number: 1
Joined club: July 1995 from Mansfield
League Games played: 126
League Goals scored: 0
International caps: 0
League Debut: 12/8/95 v Wrexham (A)

IAN BARACLOUGH

DOB: 4/12/70
Position: Defender
Usual shirt number: 6
Joined club: October 1995 from Mansfield
League Games played: 111
League Goals scored: 10
International caps: 0
League Debut: 14/10/95 v Rotherham United (H)

IAN HENDON

DOB: 5/12/71
Position: Defender
Usual shirt number: 2
Joined club: February 1997 from Leyton Orient
League Games played: 50
League Goals scored: 0
International caps: 0
League Debut: 25/2/97 v Millwall (A)

ACTION IMAGES

Darren Ward: winning a division isn't always about goals – it's clean sheets, too

Ian Rendon in action against Barnet, 7/3/98

ACTION IMAGES

GRAEME HOGG

DOB: 17/6/64
Position: Defender
Usual shirt number: 12
Joined club: January 1995 from Hearts
League Games played: 66
League Goals scored: 0
International caps: 0
League Debut: 31/1/95 v Stoke (A) Anglo-Italian Cup semi-final second leg

DENNIS PEARCE

DOB: 10/9/74
Position: Defender
Usual shirt number: 3
Joined club: July 1997 from Wolverhampton Wanderers
League Games played: 38
League Goals scored: 1
International caps: 0
League Debut: 9/8/97 v Rochdale (H)

MATTHEW REDMILE

DOB: 12/11/76
Position: Defender
Usual shirt number: 4
Joined club: July 1995 from trainee
League Games played: 57
League Goals scored: 5
International caps: 0
League Debut: 20/12/96 v Crewe Alexandra (A)

GARY STRODDER

DOB: 1/4/65
Position: Defender
Usual shirt number: 5
Joined club: July 1995 from West Bromwich Albion
League Games played: 110
League Goals scored: 9
International caps: 0
League Debut: 12/8/95 v Wrexham (A)

Phil Robinson: into the third season of his second stint with the Magpies, hard work has earned its reward

ACTION IMAGES

ALEX DYER
DOB: 14/11/65
Position: Midfielder
Usual shirt number: 6
Joined club: March 1998 from Huddersfield Town
League Games played: 10
League Goals scored: 0
International caps: 0
League Debut: 3/3/98 v Exeter City (A)

IAN RICHARDSON
DOB: 22/10/70
Position: Midfielder
Usual shirt number: 8
Joined club: January 1996 from Birmingham City
League Games played: 64
League Goals scored: 2
International caps: 0
League Debut: 20/1/96 v Wrexham (H)

SHAUN CUNNINGTON
DOB: 4/1/66
Position: Midfielder
Usual shirt number: 12
Joined club: March 1997 from West Bromwich Albion
League Games played: 17
League Goals scored: 0
International caps: 0
League Debut: 15/3/97 v Rotherham United (A)

SHAUN DERRY
DOB: 6/12/77
Position: Midfielder
Usual shirt number: 6
Joined club: April 1996 from trainee
League Games played: 79
League Goals scored: 4
International caps: 0
League Debut: 12/3/96 v York City (H)

PHIL ROBINSON
DOB: 6/1/67
Position: Midfielder
Usual shirt number: 8
Joined club: August 1989 from Wolverhampton Wanderers and August 1996 from Chesterfield
League Games played: 143
League Goals scored: 10
International caps: 0
League Debut: 19/8/89 v Leyton Orient (A)

MARK ROBSON
DOB: 22/5/69
Position: Midfielder
Usual shirt number: 11
Joined club: From Charlton in July 1997
League Games played: 28
League Goals scored: 3
International caps: 0
League Debut: 1997/98 season

Midfielder Mark Robson will be looking to improve his 3-goal tally of last season

Action Images

STEVE FINNAN

DOB: 20/4/76
Position: Striker
Usual shirt number: 7
Joined club: March 1996 from Birmingham City
League Games played: 64
League Goals scored: 5
International caps: 0
League Debut: 6/3/96 v Walsall (H)

JUSTIN JACKSON

DOB: 10/12/74
Position: Striker
Usual shirt number: 9
Joined club: September 1997 from Woking
League Games played: 15
League Goals scored: 1
International caps: 0
League Debut: 18/10/97 v Swansea City (A)

CRAIG DUDLEY

DOB: 12/9/79
Position: Striker
Usual shirt number: 12
Joined club: April 1997 from trainee
League Games played: 27
League Goals scored: 4
International caps: 0
League Debut: 15/3/97 v Rotherham United (H)

SEAN FARRELL

DOB: 28/2/69
Position: Striker
Usual shirt number: 9
Joined club: October 1996 from Peterborough United
League Games played: 49
League Goals scored: 16
International caps: 0
League Debut: 15/10/96 v Chesterfield (H)

GARY JONES

DOB: 6/4/69
Position: Striker
Usual shirt number: 10
Joined club: March 1996 from Southend United
League Games played: 89
League Goals scored: 32
International caps: 0
League Debut: 2/3/96 v Hull City (H)

GARY MARTINDALE

DOB: 24/6/71
Position: Striker
Usual shirt number: 12
Joined club: March 1996 from Peterborough United
League Games played: 66
League Goals scored: 13
International caps: 0
League Debut: 9/3/96 v Blackpool (A)

ALL-TIME RECORDS

1997/98 SEASON FINAL POSITIONS

POINTS 10 20 30 40 50 60 70 80 90 100 200 300 400 500

Club	Points	Goals	Position in Division Two at start of 1998/99 season	Average position by points in the league since joining	Average position by goals in the league since joining
AFC Bournemouth	3360	4141	9	58	70
Blackpool	4004	5466	12	25	27
Bristol Rovers	3437	4600	5	51	48
Burnley	4315	5995	20	12	16
Chesterfield	3794	4983	10	34	39
Colchester United	2378	3021	24	82	81
Fulham	3643	5006	6	39	36
Gillingham	3127	3890	8	70	76
Lincoln City	3908	5642	23	30	25
Luton Town	3404	4788	17	54	42
Macclesfield Town	99	82	22	92	92
Manchester City	4250	6219	1	17	10
Millwall	3523	4454	18	42	59
Northampton Town	3404	4740	4	55	43
Notts County	4270	5848	21	16	18
Oldham Athletic	3674	5003	13	37	37
Preston North End	4345	6014	15	9	14
Reading	3604	4795	3	40	41
Stoke City	3830	5048	2	33	35
Walsall	3468	4903	19	46	40
Wigan Athletic	1256	1260	11	87	87
Wrexham	3378	4651	7	56	46
Wycombe Wdrs	323	292	14	91	91
York City	2940	4032	16	75	72

3 Position in Division Two at start of 1998/99 season

92 Average position by points in the league since joining (includes 2 points for a win and 3 points for a win)

92 Average position by goals in the league since joining

1 Watford (p)
2 Bristol City (p)
3 Grimsby Town (p)
4 Northampton Town
5 Bristol Rovers
6 Fulham
7 Wrexham
8 Gillingham
9 AFC Bournemouth
10 Chesterfield Town
11 Wigan Athletic
12 Blackpool
13 Oldham Athletic
14 Wycombe Wdrs
15 Preston North End
16 York City
17 Luton Town
18 Millwall
19 Walsall
20 Burnley
21 Brentford (r)
22 Plymouth Argyle (r)
23 Carlisle United (r)
24 Southend United (r)

Notts County's total points since joining league 4270

Meadow Lane: home of Notts County
AEROFILMS

SUPERCLUBS
UNOFFICIAL
SOCCER YEARBOOK 98/99

JULY 1998 – JUNE 1999 DIARY AND CLUB FIXTURES

Fixture dates are subject to change. FA Cup draws were not made at the time of going to press. Worthington Cup draws are given where known at press time.

THE STORY OF DIVISION TWO SOCCER IN THE 1997/98 SEASON

FOR SUPPORTERS OF

NOTTS COUNTY

DIVISION TWO CLUB ADDRESSES

AFC BOURNEMOUTH
Dean Court Ground, Bournemouth, Dorset, BH7 7AF
Main No: 01202 395381

BLACKPOOL
Bloomfield Road Ground, Blackpool, FY1 6JJ
Main No: 01253 404331

BRISTOL ROVERS
The Memorial Ground, Filton Avenue, Horfield, Bristol, BS7 OAQ
Main No: 0117 977 2000

BURNLEY
Turf Moor, Burnley, Lancashire, BB10 4BX
Main No: 01282 700 000

CHESTERFIELD
Recreation Ground, Saltergate, Chesterfield, S40 4SX
Main No: 01246 209 765

COLCHESTER UNITED
Layer Road Ground, Colchester, Essex, CO2 7JJ
Main No: 01206 508 800

FULHAM
Craven Cottage, Stevenage Road, Fulham, London, SW6 6HH
Main No: 0171 736 6561

GILLINGHAM TOWN
Priestfield Stadium, Redfern Avenue, Gillingham, Kent, ME7 4DD
Main No: 01634 851 854

LINCOLN CITY
Sincil Bank, Lincoln, LN5 8LD
Main No: 01522 880 011

LUTON TOWN
Kenilworth Road Stadium, 1 Maple Road, Luton, Beds, LU4 8AW
Main No: 01582 411 622

MACCLESFIELD TOWN
The Moss Rose Ground, London Road, Macclesfield, Cheshire
Main No: 01625 264 686

MANCHESTER CITY
Maine Road, Moss Side, Manchester, M14 7WN
Main No: 0161 224 5000

MILLWALL
Millwall Football & Athletic Co (1985) plc, The Den, Zampa Road, Bermondsey, London SE16 3LN
Main No: 232 1222

NORTHAMPTON TOWN
Sixfields Stadium, Upton Way, Northampton, NN5 5QA
Main No: 01604 757 773

NOTTS COUNTY
County Ground, Meadow Lane, Nottingham, NG2 3HJ
Main No: 0115 952 9000

OLDHAM ATHLETIC
Boundary Park, Oldham, Lancashire, OL1 2PA
Main No: 0161 624 4972

PRESTON NORTH END
Deepdale, Preston, Lancashire, PR1 6RU
Main No: 01772 902 020

READING
Elm Park, Norfolk Road, Reading, RG30 2EF
Main No: 01189 507 878

STOKE CITY
Victoria Ground, Stoke-on-Trent, Staffordshire, ST4 4EG
Main No: 01782 592 222

WALSALL
Bescot Stadium, Bescot Crescent, Walsall, WS1 4SA
Main No: 01922 622 791

WIGAN ATHLETIC
Springfield Park, Wigan, WN6 7BA
Main No: 01942 244 433

WREXHAM
Racecourse Ground, Mold Road, Wrexham, LL11 2AH
Main No: 01978 262 129

WYCOMBE WANDERERS
Adams Park, Hillbottom Road, Sands, High Wycombe, Bucks, HP12 4HJ
Main No: 01494 472 100

YORK CITY
Bootham Crescent, York, YO3 7AQ
Main No: 01904 624 447

ALL-CLUB LOCATIONS

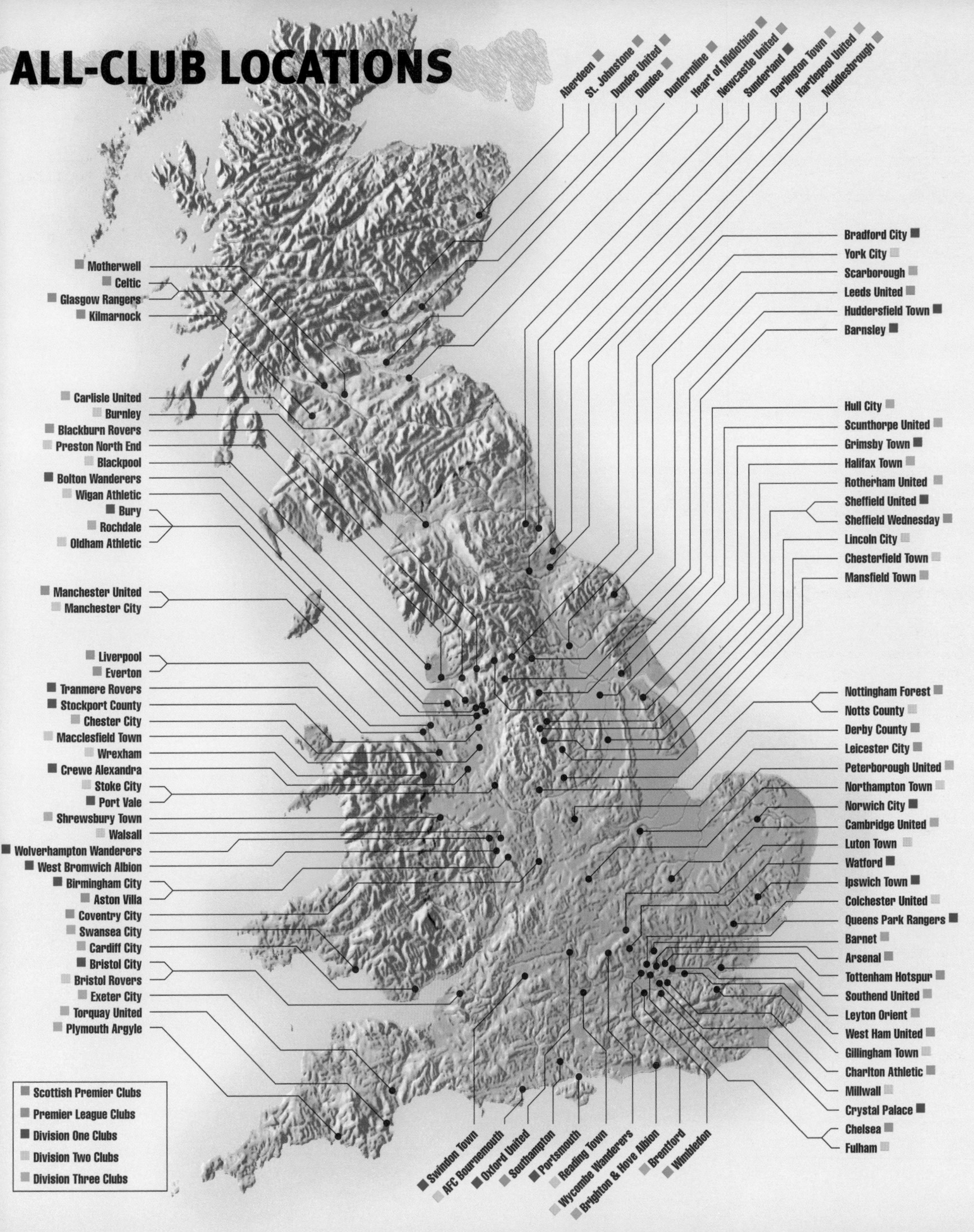

CALENDAR 1998

January

	M	T	W	T	F	S	S
1				1	2	3	4
2	5	6	7	8	9	10	11
3	12	13	14	15	16	17	18
4	19	20	21	22	23	24	25
5	26	27	28	29	30	31	

February

	M	T	W	T	F	S	S
5							1
6	2	3	4	5	6	7	8
7	9	10	11	12	13	14	15
8	16	17	18	19	20	21	22
9	23	24	25	26	27	28	

March

	M	T	W	T	F	S	S
9							1
10	2	3	4	5	6	7	8
11	9	10	11	12	13	14	15
12	16	17	18	19	20	21	22
13	23	24	25	26	27	28	29
14	30	31					

April

	M	T	W	T	F	S	S
14			1	2	3	4	5
15	6	7	8	9	10	11	12
16	13	14	15	16	17	18	19
17	20	21	22	23	24	25	26
18	27	28	29	30			

May

	M	T	W	T	F	S	S
18					1	2	3
19	4	5	6	7	8	9	10
20	11	12	13	14	15	16	17
21	18	19	20	21	22	23	24
22	25	26	27	28	29	30	31

June

	M	T	W	T	F	S	S
23	1	2	3	4	5	6	7
24	8	9	10	11	12	13	14
25	15	16	17	18	19	20	21
26	22	23	24	25	26	27	28
27	29	30					

July

	M	T	W	T	F	S	S
27			1	2	3	4	5
28	6	7	8	9	10	11	12
29	13	14	15	16	17	18	19
30	20	21	22	23	24	25	26
31	27	28	29	30	31		

August

	M	T	W	T	F	S	S
31						1	2
32	3	4	5	6	7	8	9
33	10	11	12	13	14	15	16
34	17	18	19	20	21	22	23
35	24	25	26	27	28	29	30
36	31						

September

	M	T	W	T	F	S	S
36		1	2	3	4	5	6
37	7	8	9	10	11	12	13
38	14	15	16	17	18	19	20
39	21	22	23	24	25	26	27
40	28	29	30				

October

	M	T	W	T	F	S	S
40				1	2	3	4
41	5	6	7	8	9	10	11
42	12	13	14	15	16	17	18
43	19	20	21	22	23	24	25
44	26	27	28	29	30	31	

November

	M	T	W	T	F	S	S
44							1
45	2	3	4	5	6	7	8
46	9	10	11	12	13	14	15
47	16	17	18	19	20	21	22
48	23	24	25	26	27	28	29
49	30						

December

	M	T	W	T	F	S	S
49		1	2	3	4	5	6
50	7	8	9	10	11	12	13
51	14	15	16	17	18	19	20
52	21	22	23	24	25	26	27
53	28	29	30	31			

UK Holiday Scotland Holiday N. Ireland Holiday Not in Scotland

CALENDAR 1999

January

	M	T	W	T	F	S	S
1					1	2	3
2	4	5	6	7	8	9	10
3	11	12	13	14	15	16	17
4	18	19	20	21	22	23	24
5	25	26	27	28	29	30	31

February

	M	T	W	T	F	S	S
6	1	2	3	4	5	6	7
7	8	9	10	11	12	13	14
8	15	16	17	18	19	20	21
9	22	23	24	25	26	27	28

March

	M	T	W	T	F	S	S
10	1	2	3	4	5	6	7
11	8	9	10	11	12	13	14
12	15	16	17	18	19	20	21
13	22	23	24	25	26	27	28
14	29	30	31				

April

	M	T	W	T	F	S	S
14				1	2	3	4
15	5	6	7	8	9	10	11
16	12	13	14	15	16	17	18
17	19	20	21	22	23	24	25
18	26	27	28	29	30		

May

	M	T	W	T	F	S	S
18						1	2
19	3	4	5	6	7	8	9
20	10	11	12	13	14	15	16
21	17	18	19	20	21	22	23
22	24	25	26	27	28	29	30
23	31						

June

	M	T	W	T	F	S	S
23		1	2	3	4	5	6
24	7	8	9	10	11	12	13
25	14	15	16	17	18	19	20
26	21	22	23	24	25	26	27
27	28	29	30				

July

	M	T	W	T	F	S	S
27				1	2	3	4
28	5	6	7	8	9	10	11
29	12	13	14	15	16	17	18
30	19	20	21	22	23	24	25
31	26	27	28	29	30	31	

August

	M	T	W	T	F	S	S
31							1
32	2	3	4	5	6	7	8
33	9	10	11	12	13	14	15
34	16	17	18	19	20	21	22
35	23	24	25	26	27	28	29
36	30	31					

September

	M	T	W	T	F	S	S
36			1	2	3	4	5
37	6	7	8	9	10	11	12
38	13	14	15	16	17	18	19
39	20	21	22	23	24	25	26
40	27	28	29	30			

October

	M	T	W	T	F	S	S
40					1	2	3
41	4	5	6	7	8	9	10
42	11	12	13	14	15	16	17
43	18	19	20	21	22	23	24
44	25	26	27	28	29	30	31

November

	M	T	W	T	F	S	S
45	1	2	3	4	5	6	7
46	8	9	10	11	12	13	14
47	15	16	17	18	19	20	21
48	22	23	24	25	26	27	28
49	29	30					

December

	M	T	W	T	F	S	S
49			1	2	3	4	5
50	6	7	8	9	10	11	12
51	13	14	15	16	17	18	19
52	20	21	22	23	24	25	26
53	27	28	29	30	31		

Monday June 29 1998

Tuesday June 30 1998

Wednesday July 1 1998

Thursday July 2 1998

Friday July 3 1998

Saturday July 4 1998

Sunday July 5 1998

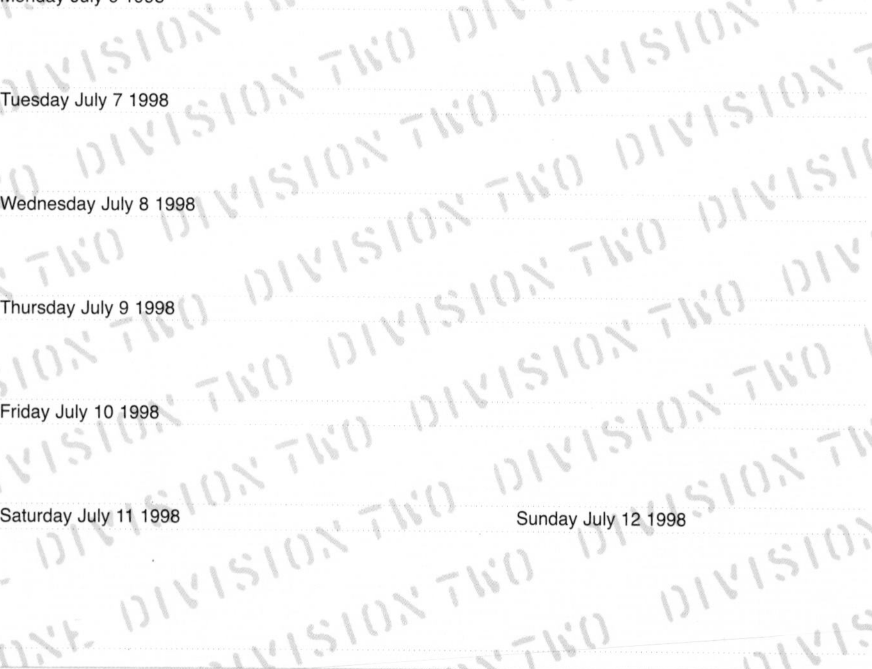

Monday July 6 1998

Tuesday July 7 1998

Wednesday July 8 1998

Thursday July 9 1998

Friday July 10 1998

Saturday July 11 1998

Sunday July 12 1998

One of the pre-season favourites for the Second Division, Millwall, lived up to expectations by beating local rivals Brentford 3–0 on the first day of the season at the New Den. Having endured near bankruptcy and savage cost-cutting the year before, ending ultimately in relegation from the First Division, Billy Bonds' Millwall went ahead before half-time thanks to an own goal by Brentford defender Bates. Further goals followed after the break through Sadlier and Grant, and Millwall sent most of the near capacity 9,000 crowd home happy and confident of an immediate return to the First Division.

ALLSPORT

Billy Bonds: sending Millwall fans home happy

Watford started the new season under Elton John and Graham Taylor, determined to make it out of the Second Division and create the 'new dawn' at the Hertfordshire club, and a 1–0 win over Burnley gave them the perfect start. Led by ex-Nottingham Forest striker (and target of many 'Pineapple' jibes) Jason Lee, and former Celtic and West Ham winger Stuart Slater, Watford swarmed all over Burnley, missing chance after chance before Lee poked a shot home on the half-hour on his debut for the club. More chances followed, but Chris Waddle's Burnley never really threatened and Watford held out for the victory they deserved.

ACTION IMAGES

Looking for a good season ahead, Watford's Jason Lee in goalscoring form

Monday July 13 1998

Tuesday July 14 1998

Wednesday July 15 1998

Thursday July 16 1998

Friday July 17 1998

Saturday July 18 1998

Sunday July 19 1998

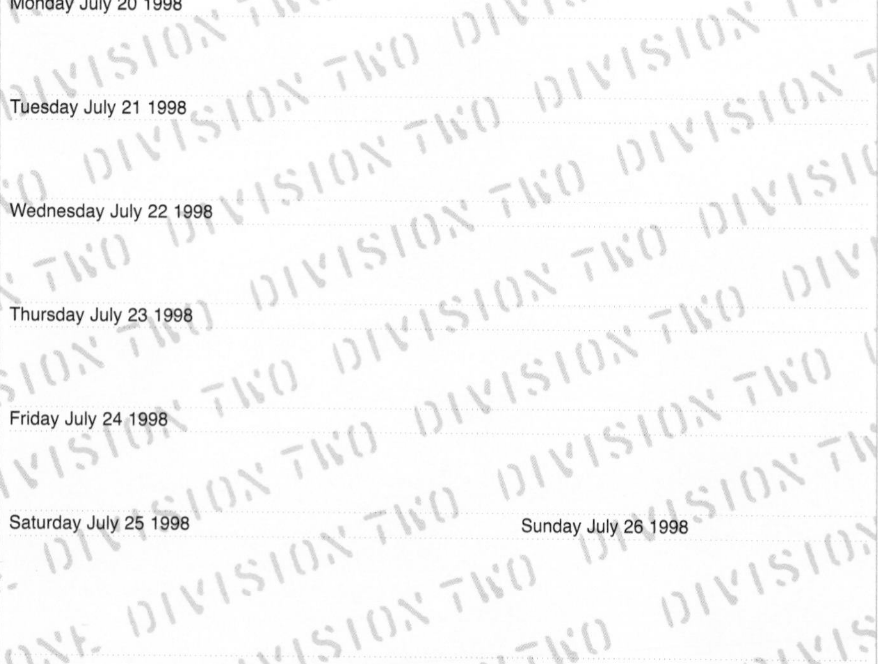

Monday July 20 1998

Tuesday July 21 1998

Wednesday July 22 1998

Thursday July 23 1998

Friday July 24 1998

Saturday July 25 1998

Sunday July 26 1998

9,341 people packed into Bristol City's Ashton Gate ground in the second week of August to see 90 minutes of tempestuous Coca-Cola Cup football against hated rivals Bristol Rovers. But despite the best efforts of both teams, each goal-line led a charmed life and the first leg of this first round tie ended 0–0. Rovers went close on a number of occasions, with Jamie Cureton hitting the bar, but could count themselves lucky after the referee missed a punch by Barry Hayles on a City defender – just the sort of passion that the locals didn't want to see in a game like this.

Action Images

Mark Blake joined Fulham's star roster free from Shrewsbury in 1994

Northampton Town beat Luton to go third in the Second Division table, a result that left the Bedfordshire side a point off the relegation zone. Parrish scored the only goal of the game after two minutes, and despite their best efforts, Luton were unable to get an equaliser, much to the delight of the 7,246 crowd at the Sixfields Stadium. Their cause was not helped by referee Harris sending off of McGowan after 44 minutes. The result pushed Northampton to within two points of runaway leaders Watford, and left Luton looking strongly at the possibility of a second consecutive relegation.

Williams and Butler of Burnley and Gillingham get to grips with the new campaign

ALLSPORT

Monday July 27 1998

Tuesday July 28 1998

Wednesday July 29 1998

Thursday July 30 1998

Friday July 31 1998

Saturday August 1 1998

Sunday August 2 1998

Luton's Dwight Marshall proved a constant thorn in Southend's side as two of the teams expected to be challenging for promotion met at Kenilworth Road. But neither played well enough to justify their position as pre-season title challengers. Only a late goal from substitute Stuart Douglas gave Luton the win. Marshall ran the Southend defence ragged, and Luton missed a few chances, but overall neither side showed why they were fancied for a quick return to the First Division. Already manager Lenny Lawrence was worrying about declining attendances at Luton as the side struggled to challenge for promotion.

ACTION IMAGES

Karl Connelly of Wrexham in action against Fulham, 9/8/97

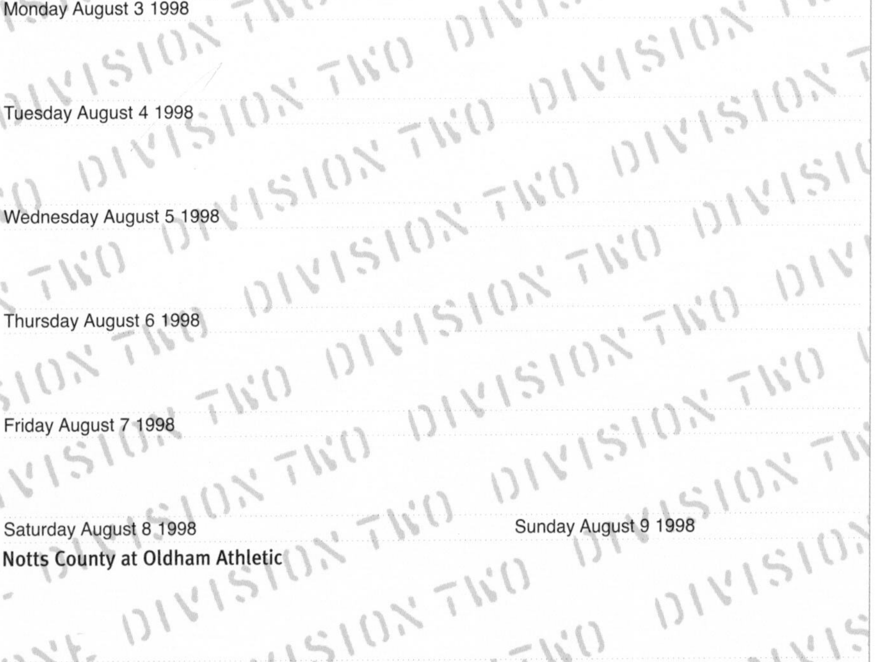

Monday August 3 1998

Tuesday August 4 1998

Wednesday August 5 1998

Thursday August 6 1998

Friday August 7 1998

Saturday August 8 1998
Notts County at Oldham Athletic

Sunday August 9 1998

Despite not scoring, ex-Liverpool and Tottenham striker Ronny Rosenthal gave a superb debut performance as Watford recorded their fourth win in four straight games to stay clear at the top of the Second Division. Rosenthal helped set up first-half goals for Keith Millen and Danish trialist Lars Melvang, as Watford swept into a 2–0 lead inside the first 11 minutes. Taylor pulled one back for Brentford from the penalty spot with 15 minutes left, but Graham Taylor's high-flyers sealed the victory with a superb third goal near the end, from Richard Johnson, to reaffirm their position as title favourites.

The man from the Premier: Ronny Rosenthal helps keep Watford at the top

ACTION IMAGES

Monday August 10 1998

Tuesday August 11 1998
Worthington Cup 1(1)

Wednesday August 12 1998

Thursday August 13 1998

Friday August 14 1998

Saturday August 15 1998
AFC Bournemouth at Notts County

Sunday August 16 1998

Monday August 17 1998

Tuesday August 18 1998
Worthington Cup 1(2)

Wednesday August 19 1998

Thursday August 20 1998

Friday August 21 1998

Saturday August 22 1998
Notts County at Northampton Town

Sunday August 23 1998

A strong performance by David Linnighan and the rest of the Blackpool team helped the Lancashire club to a famous win on penalties over Manchester City in the Coca-Cola Cup. Conceding a late goal to Kevin Horlock to lose 1–0 on the night with the tie level at 1–1, Nigel Worthington's side proved the stronger against a side containing Kinkladze, Rosler, and £3.5 million Lee Bradbury, with Mickey Mellon's penalty decisive in the shootout. The game ended 4–2 after the penalties, stunning the paltry 12,563 people inside Maine Road as Blackpool inflicted another embarrassing defeat on City.

ALLSPORT

Gary Parkinson helps keep Preston's end up 2–1 against Millwall, 16/8/97

Carlisle United's Matt Jansen scored two of his team's three goals as the Second Division side made their superiority pay against Third Division Chester City in the Coca-Cola Cup, and added another few pounds to his growing valuation. Carlisle maintained throughout that the young talent was not for sale, as Premiership clubs started to show more and more interest. But Jansen's powerful performances and Carlisle's struggling season increased the hype about the possibility of a deal. Liverpool and Newcastle were rumoured to be among the clubs sending scouts to check out the youngster. For the record, Carlisle won 5–1!

Tony Ellis, along with the rest of Blackpool's team strode over a stronger Man City side

ACTION IMAGES

5 September: Southend's Jerome Boere helped his side to a 3–1 win over fellow strugglers Brentford at Roots Hall, having fallen behind. Rapley scored after just two minutes to give Brentford the lead, but it lasted one minute, with former Liverpool midfielder and present-day Southend captain Mike Marsh equalising. Things settled down after the whirlwind start, but the 3,500 crowd were celebrating again after 25 minutes when Boere gave Southend the lead, followed by another goal, from Clarke, just before half-time. The second half did not live up to the first, but Southend were more than happy with 3–1 and the win.

Former Manchester United chairman Michael Knighton and his Carlisle United team failed once again in the League, away at Blackpool. This was obviously short of the form expected by their millionaire chairman and his plans for Carlisle to make it into the European Cup! Despite an 89th minute penalty equaliser by Owen Archdeacon, Carlisle still managed to concede an injury time winner as Blackpool's Clarke Carlisle scored from a near-post corner. Knighton had already had enough trouble with dwindling crowds and stories of meeting UFOs, and now his dreams of getting the unfashionable Second Division side into the Premier League seemed even less likely.

Taking Southend into the lead over Brentford, Jerome Boere scored the second goal in their 3–1 victory, 5/9/97

It's not a football, Michael, it's really a small UFO, and it's going to help get your side into the Premier League... one day

Quiz 1 About Notts County

1 Italian giants Juventus based their strip on Notts County's.
True or false?

2 Where and when was the meeting that finally gave the name Notts County to the club?
a) The George IV Hotel in December 1864
b) The George III Hotel in December 1861
c) The George V Hotel in January 1862

3 In 1947 Tommy Lawton's transfer fee was?
a) £19,500
b) £17,500 and £2,500 for another player swap
c) £5,000 and £1,000 for another player swap

Action Images

4 Notts County's first official game was played against:
a) Nottingham Forest?
b) Trent Valley?
c) Coventry City?

5 Which one of these is a Notts County fanzine?
a) Black & White and Read All Over
b) The Meadowlark
c) No More Pie in the Sky

6 Notts County's 1997 First Round FA Cup draw was against?
a) Swansea City
b) Inter Cardiff
c) Colwyn Bay

7 What was the score, in County's favour, when they played Rotherham in the Cup in October 1885?
a) 4–0
b) 15–0
c) 9–0

8 Notts County and Nottingham Forest players would regularly play in the same team. What was it called?
a) The Trent Terriers
b) Nottingham United
c) The Notts Association

9 County's manager Jimmy Sirrel had how many stints at the club?
a) 3
b) 2
c) 5

10 County's record win was?
a) 13–0 versus Nottingham Forest
b) 15–0 versus Rotherham Town
c) 12–0 versus Crewe Alexandra

Answers: 1.true 2.a 3.b 4.a 5.c 6.c 7.b 8.b 9.a 10.b

Monday August 24 1998

Tuesday August 25 1998

Wednesday August 26 1998

Thursday August 27 1998

Friday August 28 1998

Saturday August 29 1998
Manchester City at Notts County

Sunday August 30 1998

Monday August 31 1998
Notts County at Macclesfield Town

Tuesday September 1 1998

Wednesday September 2 1998

Thursday September 3 1998

Friday September 4 1998

Saturday September 5 1998
Wigan Athletic at Notts County

Sunday September 6 1998

Jan Sorensen's Second Division Walsall inflicted a humbling defeat on First Division giants Nottingham Forest in the Coca-Cola Cup second round, winning 1–0 at the City Ground. The Forest side was packed with a host of highly paid internationals, including Van Hooijdonk (Holland), Saunders (Wales) and Gemmill (Scotland). But the only goal of the game was scored by former Fulham and Bristol Rovers midfielder, Justin Skinner early in the second half. Walsall held on to beat their richer and more illustrious opponents and made it through to the next round. Only 7,841 turned up, so maybe the Forest fans knew in advance what was going to happen!

ACTION IMAGES

Humbling the giants: Walsall manager Jan Sorensen

In the shock of the round, injury-hit Premier League strugglers Coventry City visited Blackpool's Bloomfield Road, only to be beaten by a late David Linnighan goal that took the Second Division side through to the third round of the Coca-Cola Cup. In a tight match the veteran central defender scored with a quarter of an hour to go. Despite the efforts of Scotland captain Gary McAllister with Coventry teammates John Salako and Kyle Lightbourne, Blackpool held out to record a famous win and earn themselves a potentially lucrative place in the next round.

Even the talents of Gary McAllister were unable to prevent the Premiership side losing to Blackpool on 1/9/97

ALLSPORT

Monday September 7 1998

Tuesday September 8 1998
Notts County at Blackpool

Wednesday September 9 1998

Thursday September 10 1998

Friday September 11 1998

Saturday September 12 1998
Fulham at Notts County

Sunday September 13 1998

Monday September 14 1998

Tuesday September 15 1998

Wednesday September 16 1998
Worthington Cup 2(1)

Thursday September 17 1998

Friday September 18 1998

Saturday September 19 1998
Notts County at Walsall

Sunday September 20 1998

26 September: Fulham became the latest club to try and spend their way to promotion, when new owner Mohammed Fayed spent £1 million to bring Kevin Keegan in as the club's new 'chief operating officer', with Ray Wilkins as the new team coach. Fayed had spent £30 million buying the club, and wanted to attract the big name players to take the club out of 11th spot in the Second Division. Keegan also bought a five percent share in the club at the same time, and much was expected in a Division where most clubs had little money.

ALLSPORT

In the money: Kevin Keegan becomes part of a £31-million package to spend Fulham upwards

The theory that ex-stars make good managers suffered another blow, as Chris Waddle's Burnley failed to win yet again, drawing 2–2 at home with Wycombe. The team had now drawn all five of their home games, and lost all five of their away games. Despite taking an early lead against the Bucks side and then equalising in a late rally, Burnley remained bottom of the table. Waddle, like many other former stars-turned-managers, received another sharp reminder of the reality of management and continued to dream of that first win as manager. All a far cry from World Cups and European Cup finals!

Carlisle's Warren Aspinall keeps ahead of Tottenham's Sol Campbell, but it didn't stop the Permiership side winning 2–0 in their Coca-Cola Cup encounter on 30/9/97

ACTION IMAGES

Monday September 21 1998

Tuesday September 22 1998

Wednesday September 23 1998
Worthington Cup 2(2)

Thursday September 24 1998

Friday September 25 1998

Saturday September 26 1998
Millwall at Notts County

Sunday September 27 1998

Monday September 28 1998

Tuesday September 29 1998

Wednesday September 30 1998

Thursday October 1 1998

Friday October 2 1998

Saturday October 3 1998
Notts County at Wycombe Wanderers

Sunday October 4 1998

One of England's most hotly contested derbies went spectacularly wrong for Luton Town, going down 4–0 at home to Watford. Coming off the back of a bad run, Luton fans would have relished taking on the hated Hornets, but instead they had to endure four Watford goals in 29 minutes. The League leaders took pity on their neighbours after that, with no more goals, leaving Luton second from bottom. Luton's fans were less than impressed, having invaded the pitch in the first half, but they would have to wait a few months for revenge over their most passionately detested opponents.

ALLSPORT

Something to smile about: Graham Taylor gets Watford appointment

Fulham continued to collect old stars: not content with Keegan and Wilkins, ex-England World Cup player Paul Bracewell got off his Zimmer-frame and made his home debut against Blackpool. The shopping spree clearly helped the Londoners who won 2–1 to record their second victory after five defeats. But the 7,760 crowd and the comedy defending were a far cry from the glamour of Newcastle for Keegan. The talk of signing Beardsley and Mark Wright could not disguise the work needed at Craven Cottage. Burying the memory of Micky Adams, who got sacked for getting Fulham promoted, would have been a start!

ALLSPORT

The new suits at Fulham: Wilkins, Keegan, (Fayed & Co) prepare to take Craven Cottage into the big legaue

Monday October 5 1998

Tuesday October 6 1998

Wednesday October 7 1998

Thursday October 8 1998

Friday October 9 1998

Saturday October 10 1998
Lincoln City at Notts County

Sunday October 11 1998

Monday October 12 1998

Tuesday October 13 1998

Wednesday October 14 1998

Thursday October 15 1998

Friday October 16 1998

Saturday October 17 1998
Notts County at Burnley

Sunday October 18 1998

Two weeks into October – a goal from Donovan on the stroke of half-time proved enough as Grimsby Town dented Northampton's promotion charge, beating the Southern team 1–0 on the night. The defeat was Northampton's first reverse on their travels, and meant that they had blown a chance to go top of the Second Division table. They remained two points behind leaders Watford, having played a game more than Graham Taylor's men. Grimsby meanwhile pulled away from the bottom end of the table, a good preparation for their home tie against Sheffield Wednesday in the Coca-Cola Cup the following week.

ACTION IMAGES

Fulham took Oldham down 3–0 on 4/10/97. Paul Moody got two

Former Chelsea striker Steve Livingstone drove Grimsby Town's Blundell Park ecstatic as the Second Division side knocked the holders, Premiership 'giants' Leicester City, out of the Coca-Cola Cup. Having suffered the indignity of letting Ian Marshall give Leicester the lead in their first defence of the trophy, Grimsby woke up in the second half and three goals inside 10 minutes late in the game sealed a spectacular win for the small Humberside club. Half-time sub Livingstone helped himself to two goals to complete the 3–1 victory and earn his side a plum tie in the next round at Anfield against Liverpool.

Steve Livingstone goes up for the ball with Roger Nielsen in the Grimsby v Sheffield United game of 3/11/97

ALLSPORT

Russell Beardsome, formerly a Red Devil but now a Bournemouth favourite

Former Manchester United winger Russell Beardsmore helped Bournemouth to a win over cash-rich Fulham at Dean Court, and in the process struck another blow for the have-nots of English football. Having survived eight attempts by creditors to close the club down and paid off debts of £5 million, Bournemouth defeated the Londoners 2–1 in front of a bumper 7,603 crowd to go fourth in the table. Two goals by Ian Cox, both headers, sunk Kevin Keegan's newly fashionable Fulham side and showed that money does not guarantee success in football.

ALLSPORT

Big money: Paul Peschisolido in action for Fulham

New signing Paul Peschisolido, who cost Fulham a club record £1.1 million in October, scored his second goal in three games to repay some of the enormous fee Kevin Keegan paid for his services, but it was not enough to give Fulham victory in their derby at Millwall. A late goal from Paul Shaw gave the South Londoners a barely deserved draw after Fulham had controlled the whole game, and Keegan's side dropped two more points. It was the third successive game Fulham had taken the lead in and thrown it away, and the point was only their first in four away games.

ACTION IMAGES

Quiz 2 Referee Quiz

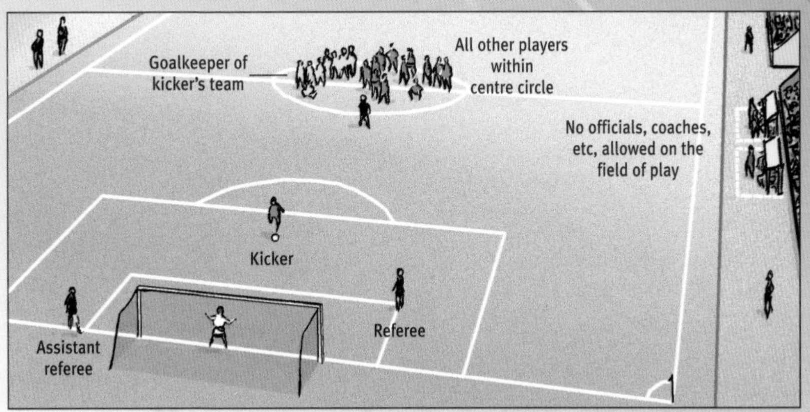

1 In the event of the crossbar being broken, or somehow moved from its position, and replacing it is not possible, the referee will:
a) Allow another item such as a taut rope to be used as a replacement.
b) Allow play to continue without a crossbar
c) Abandon the game.

2 The minimum height for a corner flagpole is
a) 1.5m
b) .5m
c) 1.75m

3 A goal is scored from a throw-in. Does the referee:
a) Disallow it?
b) Use his discretion?
c) Allow the goal?

4 Only eight players appear for one side in a professional eleven-a-side game. Does the referee:
a) Abandon the game?
b) Allow the game to continue?
c) Allow non-registered players to fill-in and continue the game?

5 An outfield player swaps positions with the goalkeeper without informing the referee. The ref notices while the ball is in play. Does he?
a) Immediately send both players off?
b) Allow play to continue and wait for a natural break?
c) Immediately book both players?

6 The ref gives a direct free kick in your penalty area. One of your players kicks it back to the keeper who misses the ball completely. The ball goes into your own net! Does the referee:
a) Order the free kick to be taken again?
b) Award a goal to the opposition?
c) Award a corner-kick to the opposition?

7 What is wrong with the picture at the top of a penalty shoot-out?
a) The goalkeeper of the team taking the kick is in the centre circle with the rest of his teammates. Should he be standing on the 18-yard line?
b) The goalkeeper has his arms raised when they should be still and by his side?
c) The referee is in the penalty area causing a distraction when he should be standing on the 18-yard line.

8 There are three minutes left in a game when one manager decides to make a substitution. Two minutes later the ball goes out of play, it takes one minute to make the substitution. Does the referee:
a) Blow the whistle for full-time when the player enters the field?
b) Book the manager for time-wasting?
c) Add time on for the substitution?

9 What is wrong with this picture of the 'Technical Area'?

a) Nothing.
b) There are no markings showing the correct distance.
c) The distances shown are wrong.

10 In this picture, does the referee:
a) Give the goal?
b) Not give the goal?
c) Give a drop-ball?

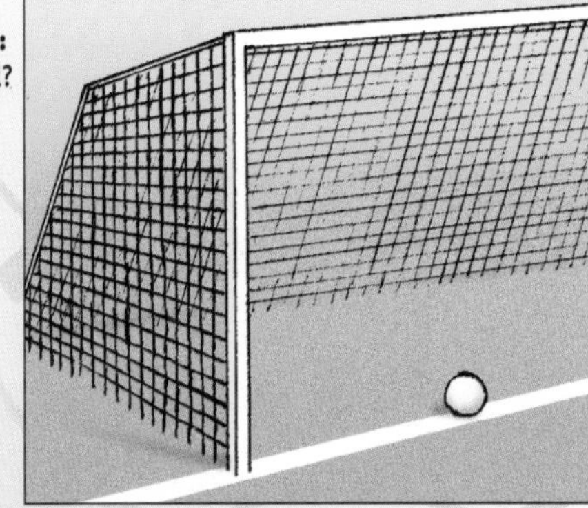

Answers: 1.c 2.a 3.a 4.b 5.b 6.c 7.a 8.c 9.a 10.b

Monday October 19 1998

Tuesday October 20 1998
Notts County at Chesterfield

Wednesday October 21 1998

Thursday October 22 1998

Friday October 23 1998

Saturday October 24 1998
Bristol Rovers at Notts County

Sunday October 25 1998

Monday October 26 1998

Tuesday October 27 1998

Wednesday October 28 1998
Worthington Cup 3

Thursday October 29 1998

Friday October 30 1998

Saturday October 31 1998
Stoke City at Notts County

Sunday November 1 1998

Watched by over 8,300 fans, Gillingham lost at home for the first time in 1997-98, against a Millwall side recovering after near-bankruptcy and a poor start. Two late goals, including one from old-timer Paul Wilkinson, gave Millwall a 3–1 win, leaving them one point off the top three with a game in hand. Gillingham's Brian Statham was sent off early in the second half for two bookable offences with the score at 0–1, but Leo Fortune-West equalised for the Kent side, before goals from Paul Shaw and Wilkinson in the last seven minutes condemned Gillingham to their first home defeat.

ALLSPORT

'Old-timer' Paul Wilkinson, here in action against Carlisle, 8/11/97

Mid November: two John Cornforth goals were not enough for Wycombe to make it through to the Second Round of the FA Cup, as the full-timers suffered the indignity of a 2–2 draw with non-league Basingstoke Town. Wycombe led 2–0 after an hour, with Cornforth getting both, but two goals within seven minutes by Coombs and Wilkinson brought Basingstoke level, with the 4,000 crowd at Adams Park left to sweat it out for the nervy last 15 minutes. The game finished 2–2, but Wycombe were left wondering if their best chance of progression had gone, faced with the prospect of a replay.

Leo Fortune-West of Gillingham has to take a knock on the home chin, along with the rest of his side

ACTION IMAGES

Monday November 2 1998

Tuesday November 3 1998

Wednesday November 4 1998

Thursday November 5 1998

Friday November 6 1998

Saturday November 7 1998
Notts County at York City

Sunday November 8 1998

Monday November 9 1998

Tuesday November 10 1998
Notts County at Luton Town

Wednesday November 11 1998
Worthington Cup 4

Thursday November 12 1998

Friday November 13 1998

Saturday November 14 1998
FA Cup round 1

Sunday November 15 1998

A classic Cup tie saw Blackpool undeservedly scrape a 4–3 win over non-league north-easterners Blyth Spartans, now managed by veteran eccentric and ex-Blackpool keeper John 'Budgie' Burridge, in the First Round of the FA Cup. Having fallen behind to a fourth minute Andy Preece goal, Blyth went 2–1 up, through Argentinian winger Di Lella. The game continued to ebb and flow, with the Seasiders going 3–2 up only to see Blyth equalise with six minutes left through substitute Jon Atkinson. But Blackpool had the last laugh with Phil Clarkson's second goal coming with one minute to go, to send the majority of the 5,000 crowd home happy.

PETE NORTON PHOTOGRAPHY

Goalscorer Steve McGavin isn't enough to save Wycombe's day

End November: despite taking the lead twice through Steve McGavin, Wycombe failed again to beat non-league Basingstoke Town, having drawn 2–2 in the first game, and went out on penalties in an FA Cup First Round replay at Basingstoke. A record crowd of over 5000 watched the Ryman League side (playing their ninth FA Cup tie of the season) equalise twice through Paul Coombs, the second a penalty six minutes from time, to cancel out McGavin's efforts. Extra time brought no further goals, and the penalty shootout saw Wycombe embarrassingly exit from the competition by 5–4 to the delight of the locals.

Crewe gave Man City a crumb of comfort as the Blues took a 1–0 home win in October

ACTION IMAGES

Monday November 16 1998

Tuesday November 17 1998

Wednesday November 18 1998

Thursday November 19 1998

Friday November 20 1998

Saturday November 21 1998
Colchester United at Notts County

Sunday November 22 1998

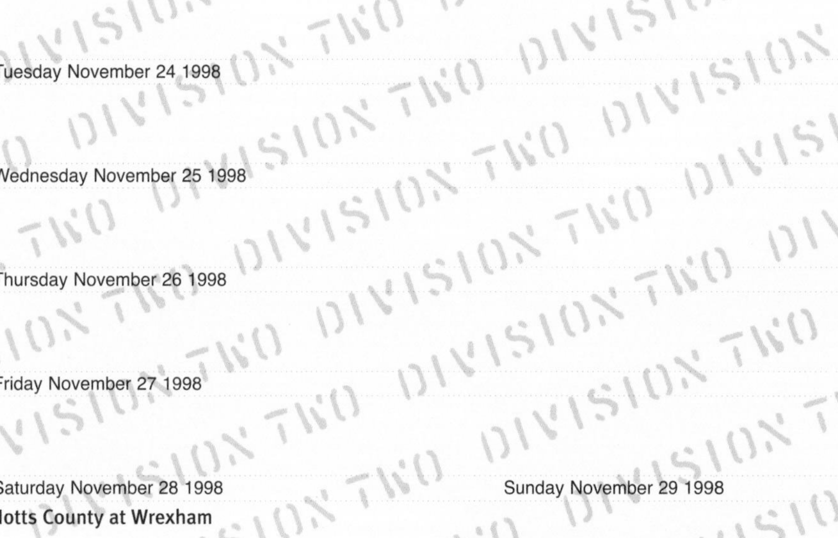

Monday November 23 1998

Tuesday November 24 1998

Wednesday November 25 1998

Thursday November 26 1998

Friday November 27 1998

Saturday November 28 1998
Notts County at Wrexham

Sunday November 29 1998

A hat-trick from Preston's Lee Ashcroft helped the Lancashire club defeat cash-rich Fulham at Deepdale, allowing Preston to leapfrog their supposedly more illustrious London rivals in the table. Fulham actually took the lead, through Scott, after just six minutes, but the advantage only lasted until the 11th minute, when Ashcroft bagged his first. The stalemate endured until the 69th minute when Ashcroft scored again, this time from the penalty spot, and again after 83 minutes to complete the win. The result left Keegan's side languishing in mid-table obscurity, and well out of the promotion frame they expected to be in.

PETE NORTON PHOTOGRAPHY

David Seal gave Northampton the lead, but not for long

A David Seal goal that gave Northampton the lead on 6 December was not enough for the Second Division side to end the FA Cup exploits of non-League Basingstoke Town. The second round tie at Sixfields finished 1–1, with Basingstoke unlucky not to win, and the non-Leaguers went home delighted with the prospect of a profitable replay. Seal had given Northampton the lead six minutes before half-time, but with 15 minutes left, Alan Carey's deflected shot gave Basingstoke the equaliser they deserved, leaving Northampton to face another game to decide who would progress to a third-round glamour tie with Leicester City.

Big London money still on the rampage: Fulham's Paul Peschisolido in action against Southend, 6/12/97

Monday November 30 1998

Tuesday December 1 1998

Wednesday December 2 1998
Worthington Cup 5

Thursday December 3 1998

Friday December 4 1998

Saturday December 5 1998
FA Cup round 2

Sunday December 6 1998

Monday December 7 1998

Tuesday December 8 1998

Wednesday December 9 1998

Thursday December 10 1998

Friday December 11 1998

Saturday December 12 1998
Preston North End at Notts County

Sunday December 13 1998

A bad day for Blackpool the second week of December, as Brentford, in the bottom four, came back from a goal down to record a vital win in their struggle against relegation. Andy Preece scored early for Blackpool, but having conceded an equaliser to Taylor on the half-hour, Blackpool pressed the self-destruct button. Malkin was sent off after 56 minutes, and five minutes later Dixon was shown the red card as well. Blackpool could not hold out, with Townley scoring Brentford's second a minute after Dixon was sent off and adding another goal with 12 minutes to go, leaving Blackpool to rue their indiscipline.

ACTION IMAGES

Northampton's Ian Clarkson in action against non-league Basingstoke

The battle of the rich chairmen at Carlisle ended in a surprising 2–0 win for the home side, with new rich kids Fulham slipping to another defeat. Two second-half goals from Stevens gave Michael Knighton's Carlisle only their fifth win all season, and moved the Cumbrian side to within a point of Burnley at the bottom of the table. Despite fielding a side including club-record £2.1 million signing Chris Coleman and the experience of Alan Neilson, Paul Bracewell and Paul Peschisolido, Fulham were beaten for the seventh time on their travels, and found themselves way down the table.

DAVE ROWNTREE PHOTOGRAPHY

Lee Hodges, on loan to Plymouth Argyle, is outnumbered by Millwall defenders, 13/12/97

Carl Heggs, Northampton's penalty scorer

Despite a replay and another 120 minutes of football at Basingstoke, it finally took a Carl Heggs penalty in a shootout to take Northampton Town through to the next round of the FA Cup. Non-league Basingstoke once again proved determined and versatile, and actually had the better chances at a frozen Camrose ground, with Alan Carey missing the best in the final few minutes. The 4,943 crowd saw no goals in extra time either, and the shootout was finally decided by Heggs, to give Northampton a lucrative and glamorous tie in the Third Round away at Leicester.

Despite goals from Allen and David Oldfield, Luton suffered another home defeat, this time at the hands of Bristol Rovers. Allen gave Luton an early lead, but Rovers scored soon after, with Cureton getting the equaliser and Hayles giving Rovers the lead. Oldfield scored immediately afterwards to level the scores, but Luton's porous defence conceded another soon afterwards, with Beadle getting the third. As if five goals in 23 minutes was not enough excitement for the 5266 crowd, Hayles scored again just before half-time to make it 4–2. The players were clearly tired out, as the second half was goaless!

Pete Norton Photography

The Equaliser: Jamie Cureton knows how to put on a celebration

QUIZ 3 ABOUT NOTTS COUNTY

1 How many times must County play Manchester City in the first month of the 1998-99 season?
- a) Once
- b) Twice
- c) Three times

2 Where was new keeper Damien Beattie born?
- a) Sydney
- b) Canberra
- c) Melbourne

3 For whom does former County player Chi-Chi Mendez play international football?
- a) Mexico
- b) Ireland
- c) Australia

BRISTOL EVENING POST & PRESS

4 Where was Mark Quayle signed from?
- a) Liverpool
- b) Everton
- c) Doncaster Rovers

5 How much did Duane Darby cost from Hull City?
- a) Nothing
- b) £5,000
- c) £15,000

6 Who was Phil Robinson signed to?
- a) Port Vale
- b) Stoke City
- c) Motherwell

7 What was County's last scoreline in Division Three?
- a) 2–2 with Rotherham
- b) 3–2 against Rotherham
- c) 5–2 against Rotherham

8 Who scored County's last goal in Division Three?
- a) Jones
- b) Farrell
- c) Robinson

9 How many points did County secure to storm Division Three in 1997-98?
- a) 100
- b) 99
- c) 98

10 How many games did County lose that season?
- a) 5
- b) 6
- c) 7

Answers: 1.b 2.c 3.c 4.b 5.a 6.b 7.c 8.c 9.b 10.a

Monday December 14 1998

Tuesday December 15 1998

Wednesday December 16 1998

Thursday December 17 1998

Friday December 18 1998

Saturday December 19 1998

Notts County at Gillingham

Sunday December 20 1998

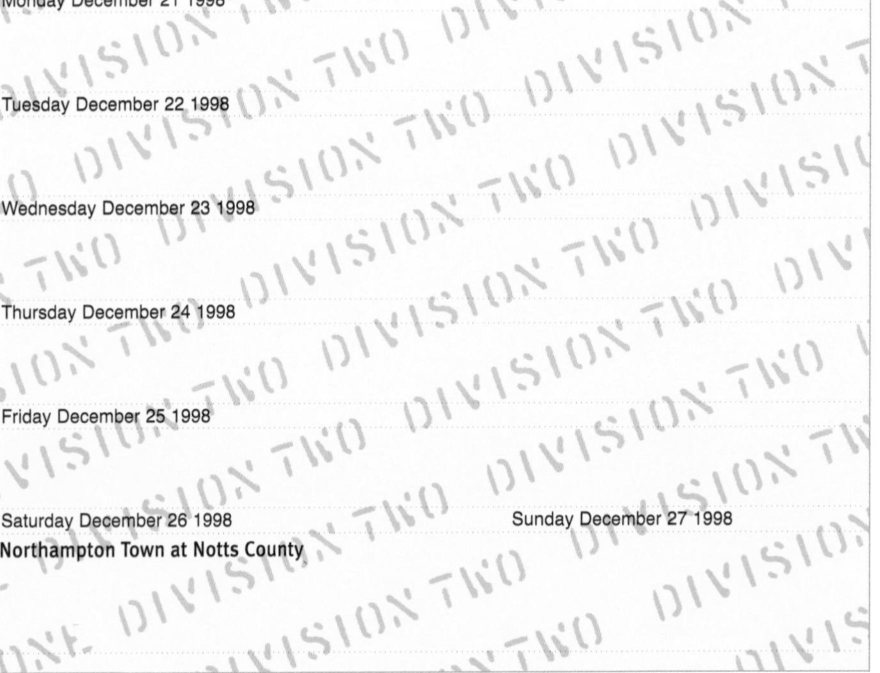

Monday December 21 1998

Tuesday December 22 1998

Wednesday December 23 1998

Thursday December 24 1998

Friday December 25 1998

Saturday December 26 1998

Northampton Town at Notts County

Sunday December 27 1998

Bristol City's Colin Cramb scored the first of his side's four Boxing Day goals against fellow promotion hopefuls Millwall, and closed the gap on leaders Watford to just two points. Two early goals from Cramb and Edwards in the first 20 minutes gave City a 2–0 half-time lead, before Carl Veart snatched one back for the Londoners early in the second half. Brian Tinnion and Taylor added two more shortly afterwards for City, however, to complete the 4–1 rout, leaving Millwall a full 19 points off the leaders and City increasingly strong bets for promotion to the First Division.

BRISTOL EVENING POST & PRESS

Aiming for the First Division: City goalscorer Colin Cramb

Bristol Rovers' Peter Beadle scored a hat-trick as Rovers thrashed Bournemouth to move to fifth in the Second Division. Goals rained in during the first half, with Bournemouth actually taking the lead through Jones after nine minutes. Beadle then sparked into action, scoring after 15 and 26 minutes, Hayles adding a third, and then Beadle sent the holiday crowd into rapture with his third in injury-time. The second half was only slightly less frantic, with Hayles scoring his second to make the score 5–1, and then Cox and Robinson restoring some pride for the out-classed south coast side.

A nice hat-trick would do: Peter Beadle in action for Bristol Rovers

Bristol Evening Post & Press

Monday December 28 1998
Notts County at Reading

Tuesday December 29 1998

Wednesday December 30 1998

Thursday December 31 1998

Friday January 1 1999

Saturday January 2 1999
Notts County at Manchester City **FA Cup round 3**

Sunday January 3 1999

Monday January 4 1999

Tuesday January 5 1999

Wednesday January 6 1999

Thursday January 7 1999

Friday January 8 1999

Saturday January 9 1999
Oldham Athletic at Notts County

Sunday January 10 1999

Watford drew with Sheffield Wednesday in the third round of the FA Cup thanks to left-back Peter Kennedy, who had been on the point of giving up professional football altogether when Watford signed him in the summer from Notts County. The draw earned Watford a deserved replay with their more illustrious opponents, and the goal was Kennedy's eleventh of the season, despite playing in defence. Wednesday had scored first through Swedish midfielder Alexandersson, but no Wednesday player touched the ball until it was already in their net, as Watford equalised direct from the kick-off.

ALLSPORT

Paul Trollope makes a run for Fulham against Plymouth, 26/12/97

Goals from Kevin Donovan, McDermott and substitute Woods helped Grimsby Town defeat First Division Norwich City in the Third Round of the FA Cup, one of the shocks of the round. Over 8,000 fans saw Grimsby take the lead from McDermott after 25 minutes, with Woods adding a second immediately after the half-time break. The presence of several experienced full internationals in the Norwich side counted for nothing, and it was Grimsby who scored again towards the end, through Donovan. The victory booked Grimsby a lucrative tie away at top division Leeds United in the Fourth Round.

Peter Kennedy celebrates his 11th goal of the season, and the one that gave Watford a third round FA Cup tie against Sheffield Wednesday. And in the second division Watford begin to dominate – apart from Burnley...

ALLSPORT

Monday January 11 1999

Tuesday January 12 1999

Wednesday January 13 1999

Thursday January 14 1999

Friday January 15 1999

Saturday January 16 1999
Notts County at AFC Bournemouth

Sunday January 17 1999

Monday January 18 1999

Tuesday January 19 1999

Wednesday January 20 1999

Thursday January 21 1999

Friday January 22 1999

Saturday January 23 1999
Macclesfield Town at Notts County FA Cup round 4

Sunday January 24 1999

The shock result of the week of 5 January saw bottom of the table Burnley beat league leaders Watford 2–0 at Turf Moor, and helped Chris Waddle's struggling side to close the gap on the teams above them in the table. Both goals came from Andrew Cooke, the first after 13 minutes, and the second after 35, and Watford's long reign at the top of the table (which they had led nearly all season) ended. Nearly 10,000 saw the surprise result, but they knew that Burnley would need a few more wins yet to get themselves out of relegation trouble.

ALLSPORT

Leicester City beats Northampton 4–0 in the third round of the FA Cup: Jason Dozzell takes on Gary Parker

Bristol City's long chase of Watford at the top of Division Two finally came off, with the win over Grimsby taking them ahead of Graham Taylor's side to first spot on goal difference. Colin Cramb put Bristol on their way with a goal after one minute, and Grimsby were clearly having a bad day in defence, conceding another in the fifth minute to Taylor, before Cramb added a third just before half-time. Goater scored again for City after 47 minutes, and Groves' consolation for Grimsby could not disguise the gap in class, though the Humbersiders could still aim for promotion.

ALLSPORT

Northampton's Chris Freestone working hard, but Premiership Leicester City make all the goal-running

Monday January 25 1999

Tuesday January 26 1999

Wednesday January 27 1999

Thursday January 28 1999

Friday January 29 1999

Saturday January 30 1999
Reading at Notts County

Sunday January 31 1999

Monday February 1 1999

Tuesday February 2 1999

Wednesday February 3 1999

Thursday February 4 1999

Friday February 5 1999

Saturday February 6 1999
Notts County at Wigan Athletic

Sunday February 7 1999

Two goals from Graham gave Oldham a priceless victory over struggling Luton at Bloomfield Road, to push the Latics into fifth place and contention for a play-off place at the end of the season. A goalless first half was quickly followed by two Oldham goals, Graham scoring after 55 and 66 minutes to give the Lancashire side a comfortable lead. A late goal from Graham Alexander gave Luton some hope of salvaging a point, but Oldham held on to consolidate their top six position, and having fallen two divisions in the 1990s, Oldham were desperate to get promoted.

Action Images

Watford's Johnson and Kennedy celebrate over Brentford, 24/1/98

Despite an 89th minute equaliser by Bull, York still managed to lose dramatically against Bristol Rovers, and leave themselves off the promotion place in the Second Division. Stephenson's early strike for York had offered hope of moving up the table into contention for a play-off position, but a Rovers equaliser from Grant straight after half-time was followed by a second goal for the visitors on the hour from Shaw. York drew level in the last minute through Bull, only for Shaw to notch his second with an injury-time winner, which meant York remained in tenth place.

Wrexham's Karl Connelly gets their second goal to make a respectable showing against Premier side Wimbledon in the FA Cup third round replay

ALLSPORT

Action Images

Preston's David Eyres is chased by Jason Lee. Watford's command increased with the 3–1 win on 17/1/98

Simon Collins' late goal capped off a spectacular second half comeback by Plymouth to transform a game they had looked sure to lose at half-time, and move the South Coast side further out of relegation trouble at the wrong end of the Second Division. Goals from Kilford and Lee inside four minutes just before the break sent Wigan 2–0 up at half-time, before strikes from Saunders and Barlow made the game level for Plymouth with 13 minutes left. Finally, Collins' dramatic winner with only four minutes left completed a memorable victory for Plymouth.

An avalanche of goals at Turf Moor saw Burnley come from behind to thrash York City 7–2, giving them renewed hope of avoiding the drop. Nearly 10,000 fans saw five Burnley goals in 18 minutes around half-time, to turn the game on its head. Pouton had scored for York, but Moore got an equaliser, and a Barras own goal and Brass made it three to give Burnley a 3–1 lead. Two more goals followed from Andy Cooke, before Barras scored at the right end for York, and then Payton and Cooke scored again to complete York's bad day.

Brentford's Glen Cockerill in action against Watford, 24/1/98

Quiz 4 About Division Two

1. **Who finished bottom of Division Two after the 1996-97 season?**
   a) Notts County
   b) Rotherham United
   c) Bristol Rovers

2. **Who was the top scorer in Division Two that season?**
   a) Shaun Goater
   b) Paul Barnes
   c) Tony Thorpe

3. **In what year did the top clubs break away from the Football League?**
   a) 1991
   b) 1992
   c) 1993

Action Images

4. **By what score did Crewe beat Brentford in the 1997 Division two Play Off Final?**
   a) 1–0
   b) 2–0
   c) 3–0

5. **A goal by Paul Smith sent which club up to Division one?**
   a) Crewe Alexandra
   b) Bristol City
   c) Luton Town

6. **Which company sponsored the Football League before Nationwide?**
   a) Carling
   b) Bass
   c) Endsleigh

7. **Which pop group provides the Theme tune for ITV's Nationwide Football League Extra?**
   a) KLF
   b)Dread Zone
   c) Blur

8. **How many clubs are there now in Division Two?**
   a) 22
   b) 24
   c) 26

9. **Who were first champions of the new Division Two?**
   a) Stoke City
   b) Birmingham City
   c) Derby County

10. **Who were Division Two champions the following year?**
    a) Shrewsbury Town
    b) Reading
    c) Norwich City

Answers: 1.a 2.c 3.b 4.a 5.a 6.c 7.b 8.b 9.a 10.b

Monday February 8 1999

Tuesday February 9 1999

Wednesday February 10 1999

Thursday February 11 1999

Friday February 12 1999

Saturday February 13 1999

Blackpool at Notts County **FA Cup round 5**

Sunday February 14 1999

Monday February 15 1999

Tuesday February 16 1999

Wednesday February 17 1999

Worthington Cup semi-finals

Thursday February 18 1999

Friday February 19 1999

Saturday February 20 1999

Notts County at Fulham

Sunday February 21 1999

A late strike for Watford by young centre forward Noel-Williams was enough to give Graham Taylor's side all three points from their trip to Chesterfield, and so steady the promotion ship following their recent erratic run. Still missing key players like Ronny Rosenthal, Watford had to rely on second-half substitute Noel-Williams, on for Thomas, to score the only goal of the game with just three minutes left on the clock. The result gave the Hornets a four-point lead at the top of the division, after Bristol City dropped two points at home.

DAVE RAOWNTREE PHOTOGRAPHY

Plymouth's Martin Barlow slides to to the tackle v Brentford, 31/1/98

Into February: Blackpool produced one of the results of the day by beating high-flying Oldham at Boundary Park, to dent Athletic's promotion hopes and take Blackpool to within striking distance of the play-offs themselves. Blackpool's poor away record, 10 defeats in 14 away games, was forgotten as Junior Bent headed home the only goal after 56 minutes. Nigel Worthington's side held on for the three points despite having Tony Butler sent off for retaliation after 69 minutes, and Oldham's Ronnie Jepson (making his debut) joined Butler early in the dressing room in injury time.

Watford's Alon Hazan, Israeli international, recovered from injury to light the midfield

Monday February 22 1999

Tuesday February 23 1999

Wednesday February 24 1999

Thursday February 25 1999

Friday February 26 1999

Saturday February 27 1999
Walsall at Notts County

Sunday February 28 1999

Monday March 1 1999

Tuesday March 2 1999

Wednesday March 3 1999

Thursday March 4 1999

Friday March 5 1999

Saturday March 6 1999
Notts County at Millwall **FA Cup quarter-finals**

Sunday March 7 1999

The relegation clash of the day saw Plymouth meet Carlisle at Home Park, and a Carlo Corazzin goal after 68 minutes proved decisive for the home side, who moved to within a point of safety. Corazzin's 12th goal of the season came with the score at 1–1, Heathcote having given Plymouth an injury-time first-half lead, and Stevens' penalty equalising for Carlisle. The result left Carlisle, who had just sold star striker Matt Jansen to Premiership Crystal Palace, deeper in trouble second from bottom, and must have been particularly depressing given the enormous distance they had to travel to get to the game.

Neville Southall's day off

Former Everton goalkeeper Neville Southall conceded another three goals during his loan period with Southend, as the Essex side crashed to their 13th away defeat of the season, at Northampton, to stay three points adrift at the bottom of the league. Goals from Freestone and Brightwell for Northampton came either side of a Boere goal for Southend before half-time, but Frain scored a third for the home side soon afterwards, the 60th goal to go into the Southend net over the season. Boere was later sent off to complete a miserable day for Southend.

Title contenders Watford fell at home to play-off hopefuls Gillingham back in February

ALLSPORT

Monday March 8 1999

Tuesday March 9 1999
Wycombe Wanderers at Notts County

Wednesday March 10 1999

Thursday March 11 1999

Friday March 12 1999

Saturday March 13 1999
York City at Notts County

Sunday March 14 1999

Monday March 15 1999

Tuesday March 16 1999

Wednesday March 17 1999

Thursday March 18 1999

Friday March 19 1999

Saturday March 20 1999
Notts County at Stoke City

Sunday March 21 1999
Worthington Cup Final

Only the second goal of his career by Paul Robinson gave league leaders Watford the lead in a typically passionate M1 derby with Luton, but a late equaliser by Johnson earned the Bedfordshire side a point. The match kicked off at noon with a heavy police presence, but the game was peaceful, and after a slow first half, Robinson gave Watford the lead on 52 minutes. But the leaders could not extend their advantage, and Johnson scored for Luton with nine minutes left, only his sixth goal in 11 years, to secure a point.

ACTION IMAGES

A surprise for Watford, Gillingham made it 2–0: this is Barry Ashby

Mid February: The battle of the relegation candidates ended in an unsatisfactory 1–1 draw between Burnley and Brentford, a result that left both teams rooted in the bottom five of the table. The draw meant that Brentford had gone 17 away games all season without a win, despite taking the lead through Taylor five minutes after half-time. That elusive first away was within sight, but with just 13 minutes left, Chris Waddle's side stirred themselves and Little grabbed the equaliser, to leave the Londoners deeper in relegation trouble – to the relief of most of the bumper 10,000 crowd at Turf Moor.

Watford goalscorer Paul Robinson

ALLSPORT

Monday March 22 1999

Tuesday March 23 1999

Wednesday March 24 1999

Thursday March 25 1999

Friday March 26 1999

Saturday March 27 1999
Notts County at Bristol Rovers

Sunday March 28 1999

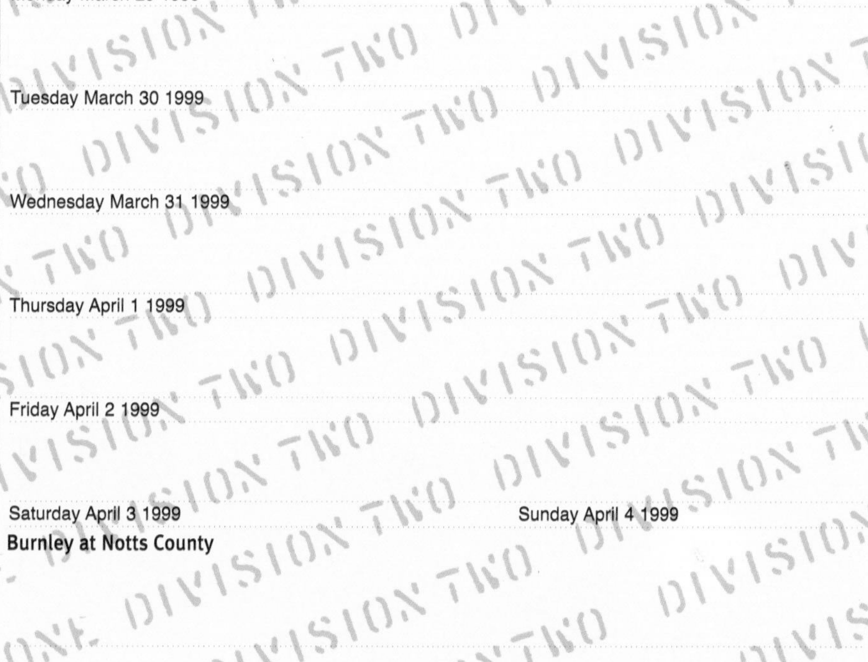

Monday March 29 1999

Tuesday March 30 1999

Wednesday March 31 1999

Thursday April 1 1999

Friday April 2 1999

Saturday April 3 1999
Burnley at Notts County

Sunday April 4 1999

Two more goals from striker Barry Hayles helped Bristol Rovers to an important win over fellow promotion hopefuls Oldham, to take his season tally to 18 in his first season of professional football. Two goals inside two minutes late in the first half put Rovers in charge, with Hayles getting the first after 43 minutes, and Tom Ramasut adding another immediately afterwards. Phil Starbuck pulled a goal back for Oldham on the hour, but another Hayles goal with 10 minutes to go sealed the victory, to take Rovers within two points of automatic promotion.

Bristol Evening Post & Press

Two more for the album: Rovers' goalscoring Barry Hayles

A sensational finish to the top game of the day with a late goal from Mooney saw Watford win the fixture against high-flying Bristol Rovers to go two points clear of nearest Bristol City. Watford had a two-goal lead by half-time through goals from Noel-Williams and Ronny Rosenthal, before White and Jamie Cureton drew City level with nine minutes to go. To the delight of most of the 12,186 crowd, Graham Taylor's men snatched a winner through Mooney with only two minutes left.

Tommy Mooney of Watford tangles with Luton's Alan Wright, 14/2/98

ACTION IMAGES

Having come from Middlesbrough only in December 1997, striker Chris Freestone earned his keep at Northampton

ALLSPORT

ALLSPORT

Peter Bearsley: a bit of strength for Carlisle?

Into March: Northampton ended a six month wait for an away victory with a win at promotion rivals Bristol Rovers in the Second Division's big game of the day, with a goal in each half. The first came from former Middlesbrough striker Chris Freestone after the half hour, and was followed by a Jason Dozzell penalty on the hour mark. The dismissal of Bishop with 11 minutes left took the gloss off their day, but Northampton could be well pleased with a hard-earned away victory that moved them into fourth and looking good for a second consecutive promotion.

A momentous day at Carlisle, where relegation-threatened Brentford secured their first away win of the season, coming from behind to win 2–1. Goals from Hogg and Stevens gave Brentford a win that took them out of the relegation zone, but the day was overshadowed by the news that former England international Peter Beardsley was watching from the Carlisle directors' box, and was expected to become player-coach at the club where he had started his career 20 years previously, signed from Wallsend for a set of kit. Carlisle chairman Michael Knighton was known to be looking to strengthen the coaching staff.

Quiz 5 Referee Quiz

1 According to FIFA, what is the minimum length of a pitch used in an international game?

a) 90 metres
b) 95 metres
c) 100 metres

2 What is the acceptable pressure of a football?

a) 0.6 to 1.1 atmospheres
b) 0.5 to 1.25 atmospheres
c) 0.75 to 2 atmospheres

3 Is the red attacking number 10 offside in this Diagram?

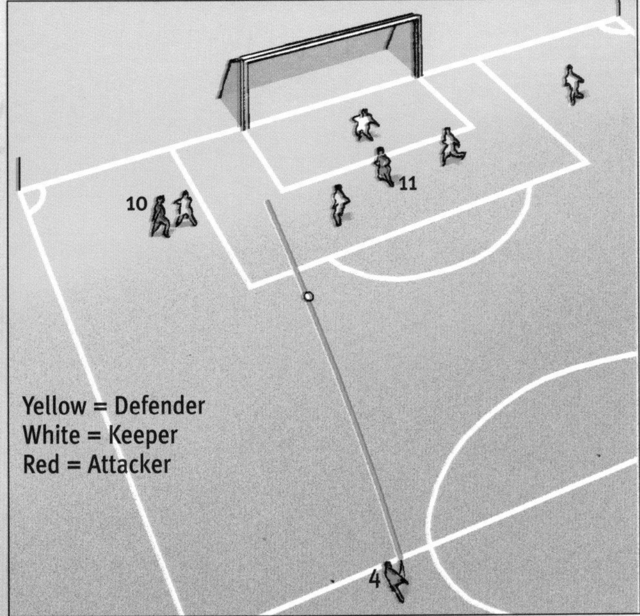

a) No
b) Yes
c) Yes, but he's not interfering with play

4 When needs to go to penalties, who decides which end they are to be taken from?

a) A toss of a coin before the game begins
b) The referee decides
c) A toss of a coin before the penalties are taken

5 If, during a penalty shoot-out, the keeper is injured and all substitutes have been used already, who replaces the keeper?

a) A substitute keeper
b) No one
c) One of the outfield players

6 Your free-kick specialist takes a corner by flicking the ball in the air and curling it into the goal. What does the referee do?

a) Awards the goal as fair
b) Awards an indirect free-kick to the opposition (the corner taker is only allowed to touch the ball once until another player touches it).
c) Awards a direct free-kick to the opposition (the corner taker is only allowed to touch the ball once until another player touches it).

7 Your keeper takes a free-kick but trips and the ball doesn't make it out of the area. What should the ref do?

a) Has it taken again
b) Allows play to continue
c) Awards an indirect free-kick to the opposition

8 An opposition player persistently stands nose-to-nose with one of your team who is trying to take a throw-in, what should the referee do?

a) Get the opposition player to stand 10-yards back
b) Award an indirect free-kick to your team
c) Caution the opposition player and give him a yellow card

9 What is the referee awarding in this Diagram?

a) An indirect free-kick
b) A corner
c) A direct free-kick

10 If an indirect free-kick goes straight into the goal, what should the referee do?

a) Have the kick re-taken
b) Award an indirect free-kick to the opposition
c) Award a goal kick

Answers: 1.c 2.a 3.a 4.b 5.c 6.b 7.a 8.c 9.a 10.c

Monday April 5 1999
Notts County at Lincoln City

Tuesday April 6 1999

Wednesday April 7 1999

Thursday April 8 1999

Friday April 9 1999

Saturday April 10 1999
Chesterfield at Notts County

FA Cup semi-finals

Sunday April 11 1999

Monday April 12 1999

Tuesday April 13 1999
Wrexham at Notts County

Wednesday April 14 1999

Thursday April 15 1999

Friday April 16 1999

Saturday April 17 1999
Notts County at Colchester United

Sunday April 18 1999

A third derby win of the season for Bristol City over Bristol Rovers took them into top spot in the Second Division over Watford on goal difference, and they became favourites for the title. 17,086 fans saw goals from Bell from the penalty spot before half-time and from top scorer Shaun Goater on the hour, which gave City the win, taking them a massive 19 points clear of their local rivals in the table. It was Rovers' fifth straight defeat, and manager Ian Holloway was disgusted by the lack of effort from certain players. City meanwhile had the title to aim for.

Bristol Evening Post & Press

Mickey Bell celebrates his goal from the penalty spot

An amazing second half at Roots Hall saw eight goals fly into the net, after a goalless first half between relegation strugglers Southend and Bournemouth. Ironically Bournemouth started the scoring just before the hour through Stein, but four goals in the next seven minutes gave Southend the points. Jerome Boere scored two and Andy Thomson scored two others, as Bournemouth were swept away. Bailey pulled one back for the visitors, but Clarke added a fifth before Fletcher scored in injury time to complete an incredible second half. The result gave Southend a better chance of avoiding the drop to Division Three, as they fought it out with Burnley, Luton and Carlisle.

Fulham's hopes slid further as Millwall beat them 2–1 on 14/3/98. This is Fulham's Tony Thorpe

ALLSPORT

Monday April 19 1999

Tuesday April 20 1999

Wednesday April 21 1999

Thursday April 22 1999

Friday April 23 1999

Saturday April 24 1999
Luton Town at Notts County

Sunday April 25 1999

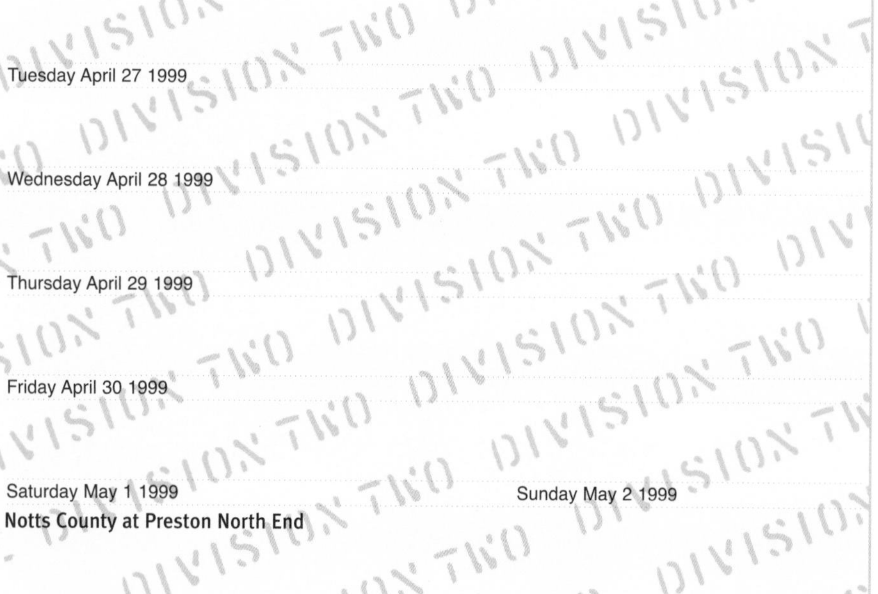

Monday April 26 1999

Tuesday April 27 1999

Wednesday April 28 1999

Thursday April 29 1999

Friday April 30 1999

Saturday May 1 1999
Notts County at Preston North End

Sunday May 2 1999

Midfielder Dave Brammer scored the crucial second goal as Wrexham continued their unlikely march into the promotion frame in the Second Division with a 2–0 win over Wycombe at the Racehorse Ground in the third week of March. Kavanah's own goal before half-time had given the unfashionable Welsh side the lead, and Brammer scored in the last minute to wrap up a win that took Wrexham into third place in the table behind season-long leaders Watford and Bristol City, and ahead of more fancied sides like Fulham and Northampton. Wycombe had won only two of their 20 away games all season.

ACTION IMAGES

Mark Stein in Bournemouth v Walsall Auto Windscreens semi-final action

The big Lancashire derby ended all square at Deepdale at the end of March, a result that suited neither Preston nor Wigan in their relegation fight. Wigan were more in need of the points and gave a debut to ex-Everton striker Stuart Barlow, but Preston scored first through Ashcroft on the half-hour mark. Wigan equalised soon after half-time through top scorer David Lowe: the striker's 15th goal of the season made him Wigan's joint top scorer of all time. The draw meant Wigan were one point clear of the relegation zone, but with two games in hand on most of the teams below them.

Burnley 0 Grimsby 2 in the other Auto Windscreens semi; Mark Robertson for Burnley and Lee Nogan

ACTION IMAGES

Monday May 3 1999

Tuesday May 4 1999

Wednesday May 5 1999

Thursday May 6 1999

Friday May 7 1999

Saturday May 8 1999
Gillingham at Notts County

Sunday May 9 1999

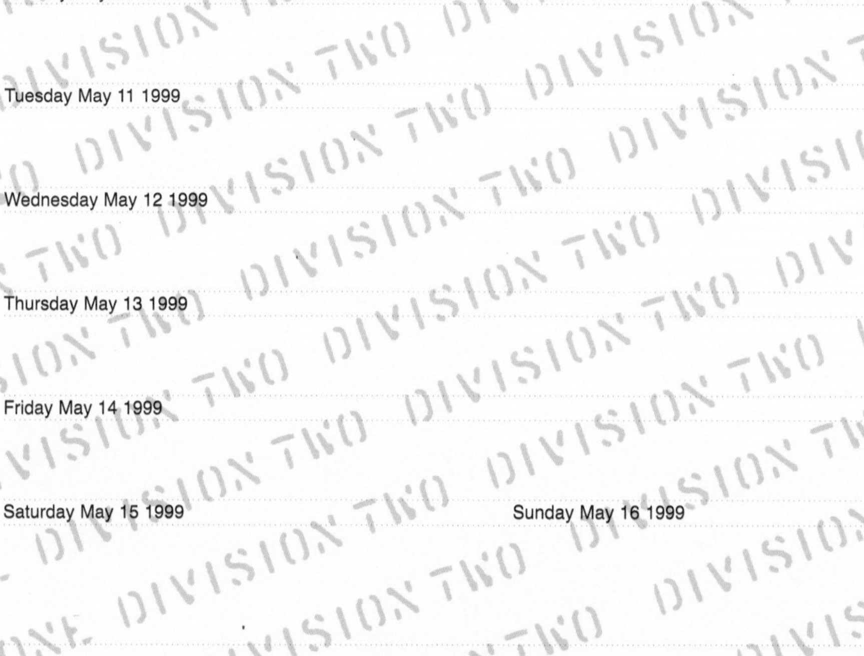

Monday May 10 1999

Tuesday May 11 1999

Wednesday May 12 1999

Thursday May 13 1999

Friday May 14 1999

Saturday May 15 1999

Sunday May 16 1999

Into April: one goal from Greg Goodridge was enough to give Bristol City a victory over struggling Carlisle United and so establish a potentially crucial lead at the top of Division Two. 12,578 fans saw Bajan striker Goodridge score just after half-time to give City the points, and make the City faithful forget the sale of striker Shaun Goater to Manchester City the previous week. City's 15th home win of the season was enough to take them four points clear of long-time leaders Watford, and made promotion to Division One almost a certainty.

LANCASHIRE EVENING TELEGRAPH

Chris Woods, young at heart and complexion, makes Grimsby miserable

Paul Moody spoiled Micky Adams' first game against his old club Fulham as Brentford went down to only their second defeat in 12 games and back in the relegation scrap. A goal from Moody midway through each half was enough to secure the points for Keegan's side, and give their chances of promotion via the play-offs a valuable boost. The win moved Fulham up to fourth and only one point behind Grimsby, with Peter Beardsley the star of the show. Adams was left to reflect on the money spent by Fulham once he had left earlier in the season.

Switching from Fulham to Brentford makes Mickey Adams moody

ACTION IMAGES

Monday May 17 1999

Tuesday May 18 1999

Wednesday May 19 1999

Thursday May 20 1999

Friday May 21 1999

Saturday May 22 1999
FA Cup Final

Sunday May 23 1999

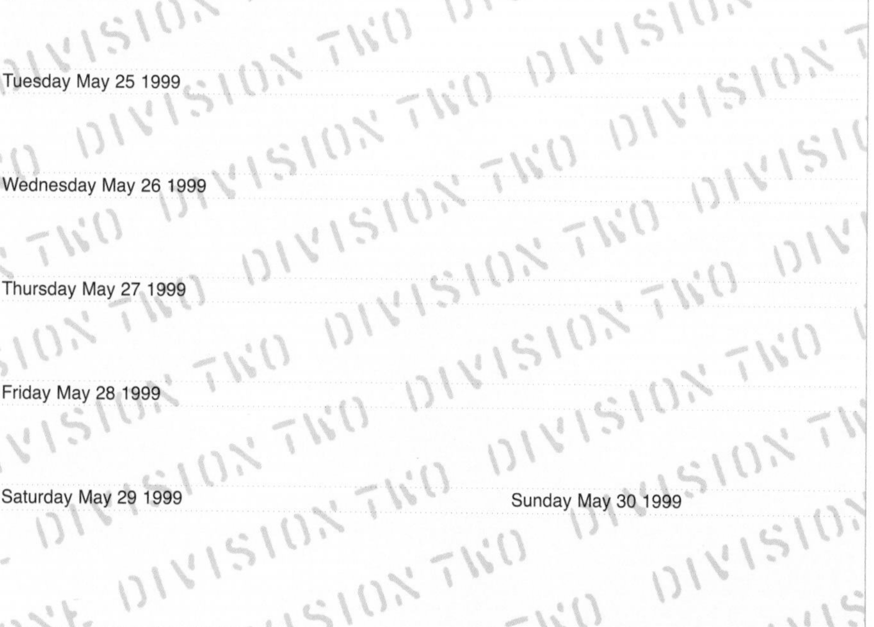

Monday May 24 1999

Tuesday May 25 1999

Wednesday May 26 1999

Thursday May 27 1999

Friday May 28 1999

Saturday May 29 1999

Sunday May 30 1999

Scenes of celebration at Wembley as Grimsby won the Auto Windscreens Shield Final on their first ever visit to the famous stadium. A Wayne Burnett goal in extra time gave the Humbersiders victory over Bournemouth, who had taken the lead through John Bailey after thirty minutes. Ex-Nottingham Forest midfielder Kingsley Black equalised for Grimsby with only 16 minutes left to play, and then Burnett popped up at a corner to flick home the winner. Despite being much derided, the final was watched by over 62,000 people, complete with inflatable haddock, and the tournament was deemed a success for another year.

ACTION IMAGES

Mark Stein tangles with Bournemouth's defence

The day's big play-off clash ended level, which did neither Gillingham nor Wrexham any favours in their promotion battle. On-loan Manchester United midfielder Mark Wilson scored his fifth goal in 13 games for Wrexham after 16 minutes, only for Akinbiyi to equalise for Gillingham just before half-time with his 20-second of the season. The result left both sides outside the promotion zone, with Wrexham in seventh and Gillingham in eighth, but given the two clubs' financial problems over the last few years, maybe the fact that either were within close to promotion at all is cause for celebration.

A Bristol-Watford sandwich: Tom Doherty, Steve Palmer, Sean McCarthy and Robert Page all play 'Spot the Ball'

ACTION IMAGES

Action Images

Grimsby Town caps a great year with a victory celebration in the Auto Windscreens Final

End of April: The battle was finally lost as Southend and Carlisle became the first sides confirmed to be relegated from the Second Division. Two late goals by Oldham at Boundary Park condemned Southend to their second relegation in three years, while a late strike by York's McMillan dashed the Carlisle hopes. Smart had given the Cumbrians belief before half-time, but an equaliser from Pouton on the hour and McMillan's goal with six minutes left meant there was no way back. Michael Knighton's dream of getting Carlisle into the Premier League by the year 2000 was suddenly looking a lot less possible.

The crucial promotion match of the day was won by one goal, as Northampton stopped Fulham from securing a place in the play-offs. Starting the day in fourth place, Fulham were unable to break down Northampton, and a single goal from Peer just before the hour gave the Cobblers three crucial points. It all but booked them a place in the play-offs, and sent Fulham to their 12th away defeat of the season. Kevin Keegan's side remained fourth with one game to play, but had blown a chance of ensuring a play-off spot and faced another anxious weekend of football.

Fulham's Wayne Collins beats Watford's Tommy Mooney, 2/5/98

Quiz 6 About Division Two

1. **When were Grimsby Town relegated to Division Two?**
   a) 1995
   b) 1996
   c) 1997

2. **Which of the following clubs were not relegated with them the same year?**
   a) Oldham Athletic
   b) Southend United
   c) Brentford

3. **Which of the following Division Two clubs was not an original member of the Football League?**
   a) Burnley
   b) Preston North End
   c) Millwall

Action Images

4. **When was the last time Luton Town Last reached the Play-offs?**
   a) 1992
   b) 1995
   c) 1997

5. **Who were promoted to Division One the Same year?**
   a) Stockport County
   b) Charlton Athletic
   c) West Bromwich Albion

6. **In what year were Watford relegated to Division Two?**
   a) 1995
   b) 1996
   c) 1997

7. **From which club did Watford's new manager come the following season?**
   a) Aston Villa
   b) Leicester City
   c) Wolverhampton Wanderers

8. **What record did Gillingham set in 1995-96?**
   a) They had six different players sent off
   b) They scored 121 league goals
   c) They conceded just 20 league goals

9. **Why did Gillingham gain entry into Division Two that season?**
   a) They were relegated from Division One
   b) They were runners-up in Division Three
   c) They won the Division Three Play-off Final

10. **During their last years in the old Division Two, Bristol Rovers played at which stadium?**
    a) Northville
    b) Westville
    c) Eastville

Answers: 1.c 2.c 3.c 4.c 5.a 6.b 7.c 8.c 9.b 10.c

Monday May 31 1999

Tuesday June 1 1999

Wednesday June 2 1999

Thursday June 3 1999

Friday June 4 1999

Saturday June 5 1999

Sunday June 6 1999

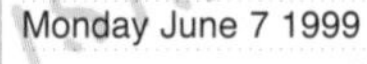

Monday June 7 1999

Tuesday June 8 1999

Wednesday June 9 1999

Thursday June 10 1999

Friday June 11 1999

Saturday June 12 1999

Sunday June 13 1999

After seemingly throwing the title away late on, a late Jason Lee goal at Fulham gave Watford the Second Division championship. The Hornets' 2–1 win over Fulham also meant that Kevin Keegan's £7 million squad still qualified for the play-offs, by finishing third. Fulham's biggest crowd for 15 years saw Paul Peschisolido miss endless chances for Fulham before young Watford star Noel-Williams tapped in a Hyde cross after 34 minutes. Peter Beardsley levelled the score early in the second half from the edge of the box, before Lee struck for Watford to ensure the Hornets finished three points clear of Bristol City.

ACTION IMAGES

Poised for anything: Rovers' keeper Andy Collett

A goal six minutes from time by Bristol Rovers' Barry Hayles sent Brentford down to Division Three and Rovers into the play-offs. A goalless first-half was only punctuated by a red card for Rovers' Gary Penrice, but the match came alive after half-time, with Jamie Cureton scoring for the home side after 50 minutes. That woke Brentford up, and with eleven minutes left, Radley equalised, only for Hayles (Rovers' player of the year) to score his 25th of the season five minutes later. Brentford paid the price for their awful away record (11 defeats) and finished two points behind Burnley.

Glory moment: Jason Lee scores the goal that makes Watford Division Two Champions

ACTION IMAGES

Monday June 14 1999

Tuesday June 15 1999

Wednesday June 16 1999

Thursday June 17 1999

Friday June 18 1999

Saturday June 19 1999

Sunday June 20 1999

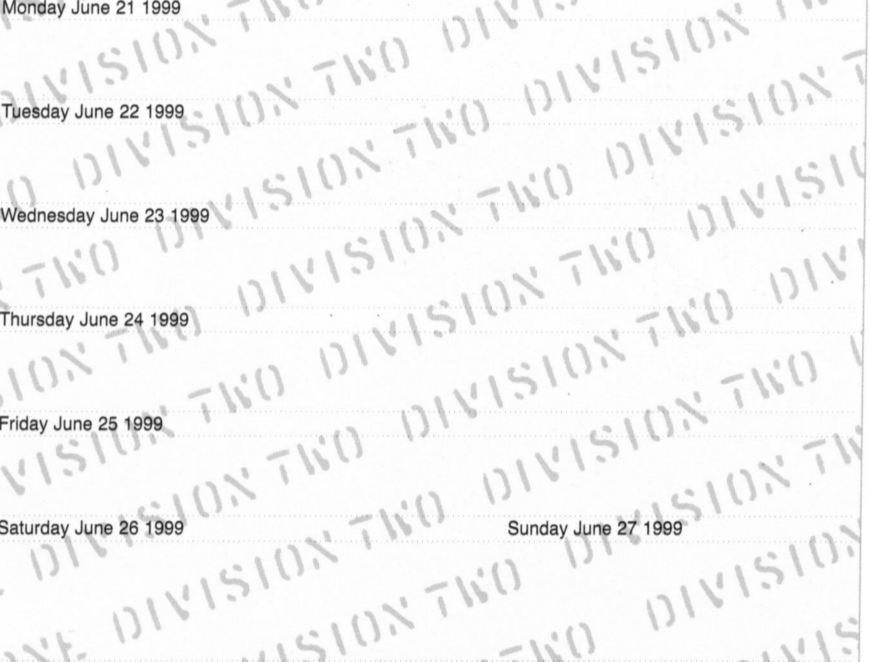

Monday June 21 1999

Tuesday June 22 1999

Wednesday June 23 1999

Thursday June 24 1999

Friday June 25 1999

Saturday June 26 1999

Sunday June 27 1999

A penalty by Bristol Rovers' Peter Beadle helped the West Country side to a significant advantage over Northampton after the first leg of the Second Division play-offs in the first week of May. First-half goals from Beagle and seven minutes later from Frankie Bennett gave Rovers a strong advantage, extended by Barry Hayles' 26th goal of the season in the second half. Having been battered by Rovers throughout the game, Northampton gave themselves a glimmer of hope of making the Wembley final late in the second half when John Gayle lobbed over the Rovers keeper, to set up an intriguing second leg.

ACTION IMAGES

It's the third Bristol Rovers goal – Gary Penrice looks happy

Grimsby took the upper hand over Fulham in the first leg of the Second Division play-off at Craven Cottage, after a 1-1 draw. Fulham had striker Paul Moody sent off for dangerous play just before half-time. But five minutes later, Fulham were awarded a dubious penalty and Peter Beardsley swept the ball in to give Keegan's men the lead. A defensive mix-up early in the second half let Smith in for Grimsby to equalise, to cap a bad week for Keegan, who 48 hours earlier had sensationally sacked team coach Ray Wilkins and taken charge of the side himself.

Peter Beardsley celebrates scoring Fulham's penalty goal against Grimsby in the semi-final first leg of the play-offs

Action Images

Monday June 28 1999

Tuesday June 29 1999

Wednesday June 30 1999

Thursday July 1 1999

Friday July 2 1999

Saturday July 3 1999

Sunday July 4 1999

Northampton Town reached the play-off final for the season, overcoming a 3–1 deficit from the first leg to beat Bristol Rovers 4–3. A record crowd at the Sixfield Stadium of 7501 saw Carl Heggs supply the early breakthrough, scoring in the first half to reduce the gap to 3–2 on aggregate. A second-half volley from Ian Clarkson on the hour and a header from Ray Warburton with 13 minutes left sent Northampton through to the final at Wembley, and the chance of a second successive promotion. Rovers were left to rue missed chances in the first leg.

Grimsby Town – a side with an interesting recent history involving Italians, managers and plates of chicken, take on Northampton Town – a team about which not a great deal has been said. That is until they rescued themselves from a 3–1 deficit to take the short journey south down the M1 to Wembley. Both teams had been in contention, and then out again, in one of the hardest fought play-off run-ins that anyone could remember. With both the top spots locked up, the battle for Wembley glory was well met. The game on the day was a tense affair, enlivened early in the 17th minute by former West Brom striker, Kevin Donovan, who was repaying the confidence shown in him by another former Baggie – manager Alan Buckley. Grimsby were on their way back to the division that they'd waved their goodbyes to just 12 months previously. But Donovan could have done better. His penalty miss in the 76th minute will not prove the nightmare it could have, but Northampton's marvellous keeper, Woodman, will feel aggrieved that his moment of glory was lost in the roar of the Grimsby crowd as the final whistle signalled the start of their celebrations.

ACTION IMAGES

Kevin Donovan celebrates scoring the first goal against Northampton in the play-off final

Peter Beadle and Ian Samson shove and push for the ball as Northampton beats Bristol Rovers to the play-off

Action Images

1998/99 PROGRESS CHART F O R S U P P O R T E R S O F

		DATE	SCORE	POINTS	PLACE	REFEREE
Notts County ....v....... AFC Bournemouth	HOME	/ /	–			
	AWAY	/ /	–			
Notts County ....v.............. Blackpool	HOME	/ /	–			
	AWAY	/ /	–			
Notts County ....v.......... Bristol Rovers	HOME	/ /	–			
	AWAY	/ /	–			
Notts County ....v .... Burnley	HOME	/ /	–			
	AWAY	/ /	–			
Notts County ....v............ Chesterfield	HOME	/ /	–			
	AWAY	/ /	–			
Notts County ....v....... Colchester United	HOME	/ /	–			
	AWAY	/ /	–			
Notts County ....v................ Fulham	HOME	/ /	–			
	AWAY	/ /	–			
Notts County ....v........ Gillingham Town	HOME	/ /	–			
	AWAY	/ /	–			
Notts County ....v .... Lincoln City	HOME	/ /	–			
	AWAY	/ /	–			
Notts County ....v .... Luton Town	HOME	/ /	–			
	AWAY	/ /	–			
Notts County ....v ...... Macclesfield Town	HOME	/ /	–			
	AWAY	/ /	–			
Notts County ....v .... Manchester City	HOME	/ /	–			
	AWAY	/ /	–			
Notts County ....v............... Millwall	HOME	/ /	–			
	AWAY	/ /	–			
Notts County ....v...... Northampton Town	HOME	/ /	–			
	AWAY	/ /	–			
Notts County ....v .... Oldham Athletic	HOME	/ /	–			
	AWAY	/ /	–			
Notts County ....v ...... Preston North End	HOME	/ /	–			
	AWAY	/ /	–			
Notts County ....v .... Reading	HOME	/ /	–			
	AWAY	/ /	–			
Notts County ....v .... Stoke City	HOME	/ /	–			
	AWAY	/ /	–			
Notts County ....v................ Walsall	HOME	/ /	–			
	AWAY	/ /	–			
Notts County ....v .... Wigan Athletic	HOME	/ /	–			
	AWAY	/ /	–			
Notts County ....v .... Wrexham	HOME	/ /	–			
	AWAY	/ /	–			
Notts County ....v .... Wycombe Wanderers	HOME	/ /	–			
	AWAY	/ /	–			
Notts County ....v .... York City	HOME	/ /	–			
	AWAY	/ /	–			

SCORERS	RED CARDS	YELLOW CARDS	COMMENTS

SUPPORTERS' AWAY INFORMATION

UNITED KINGDOM AIRPORTS

Airport	Telephone
Aberdeen (Dyce)	01224 722331
Belfast (Aldegrove)	01849 422888
Birmingham International	0121 767-5511
Blackpool	01253 343434
Bournemouth (Hurn)	01202 593939
Bristol (Luisgate)	01275 474444
Cambridge	01223 61133
Cardiff	01446 711211
East Midlands	01332 852852
Edinburgh	0131333-1000
Glasgow	0141 887 1111
Humberside	01652 688491
Inverness (Dalcross)	01463 232471
Leeds & Bradford (Yeadon)	01132 509696
Liverpool (Speke)	0151 486-8877
London (Gatwick)	01293 535353
London (Heathrow)	0181 759-4321
London (London City)	0171 474-5555
London (Stanstead)	01279 680500
Luton	01582 405100
Lydd	01797 320401
Manchester (Ringway)	0161 489-3000
Newcastle (Woolsington)	0191 286-0966
Newquay (St. Mawgan)	01637 860551
Norwich	01603 411923
Plymouth	01752 772752
Prestwick	01292 479822
Southampton	01703 629600
Southend	01702 340201
Stornoway	01851 702256
Teesside (Darlington)	01325 332811
Westland Heliport	0171 228-0181

PASSPORT OFFICES

London 0171 799-2728
Clive House, 70–78 Petty France, SW1H 9HD

Liverpool 0151 237-3010
5th Floor, India Buildings, Water Street, L2 0QZ

Peterborough 01733 555688
UK Passport Agency, Aragon Court,
Northminster Road, Peterborough PE1 1QG

Glasgow 0141 332-4441
3 Northgate, 96 Milton Street, Cowcadens,
Glasgow G4 0BT

Newport 01633 473700
Olympia House, Upper Dock Street, Newport,
Gwent NP9 1XQ

Belfast 01232 330214
Hampton House, 47–53 High Street,
Belfast BT1 2QS

TOURIST & TRAVEL INFORMATION CENTRES

ENGLAND

Centre	Telephone
Birmingham (NEC)	0121 780-4321
Blackpool	01253 21623
Bournemouth	01202 789789
Brighton	01273 323755
Cambridge	01223 322640
Chester	01244 351609
Colchester	01206 282920
Dover	01304 205108
Durham	0191 384-3720
Hull	01482 223559
Lancaster	01524 32878
Leicester	01162 650555
Lincoln	01522 529828
Liverpool	0151 708-8838
Manchester	0161 234-3157
Newcastle-upon-Tyne	0191 261-0691
Newquay	01603 871345
Norwich	01603 666071
Oxford	01865 726871
Portsmouth	01705 826722
Southampton	01703 221106
Torquay	01803 297428
York	01904 620557

SCOTLAND

Centre	Telephone
Aberdeen	01224 632727
Edinburgh	0131 557-1700
Glasgow	0141 848-4440
Stirling	01786 475019

WALES

Centre	Telephone
Cardiff	01222 227281
Wrexham	01978 292015

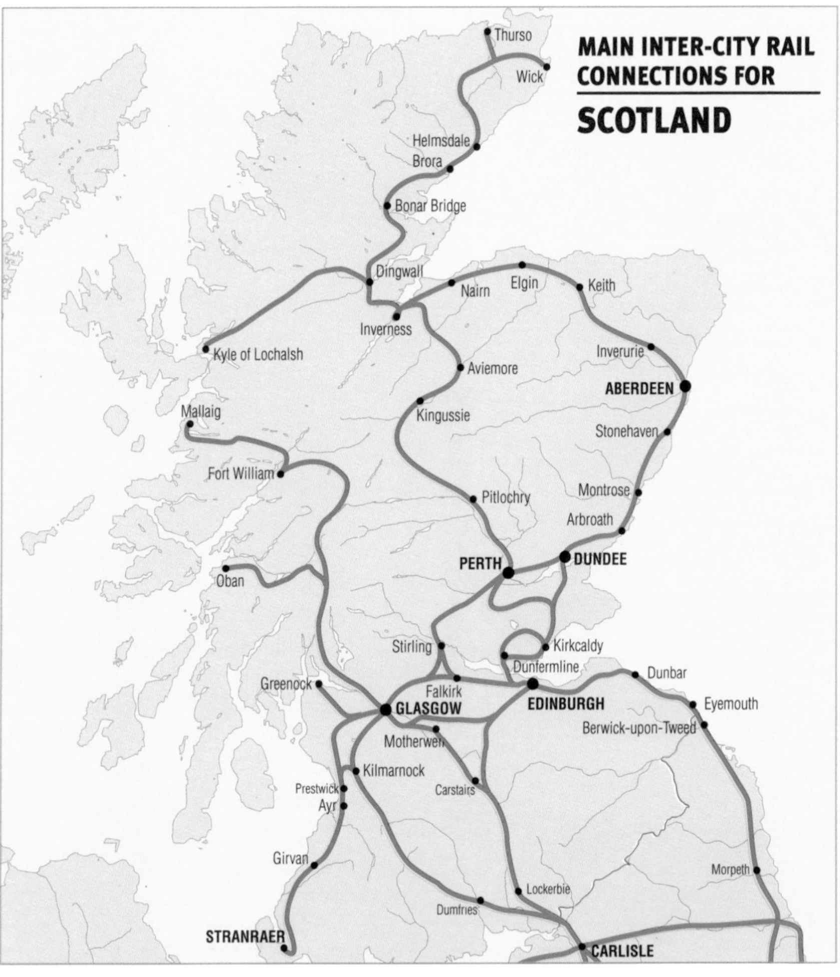

MAIN INTER-CITY RAIL CONNECTIONS FOR ENGLAND & WALES

FERRY SERVICES

B&I Line	Liverpool	0151 2273131
Brittany Ferries	Plymouth	01752 221321
Color Line	Newcastle	0191 2961313
Hoverspeed	Dover	01304 240241
North Sea Ferries	Hull	01482 795141
Olau Line	Sheerness	01795 666666
P&O European	Dover	01304 203388
P&O Scottish	Aberdeen	01224 589111
Scandinavian	Harwich	01255 240240
Stena Sealink	Ashford	01233 647047
Swansea Cork	Swansea	01792 456116

TRAIN OPERATOR CONTACTS

See following page

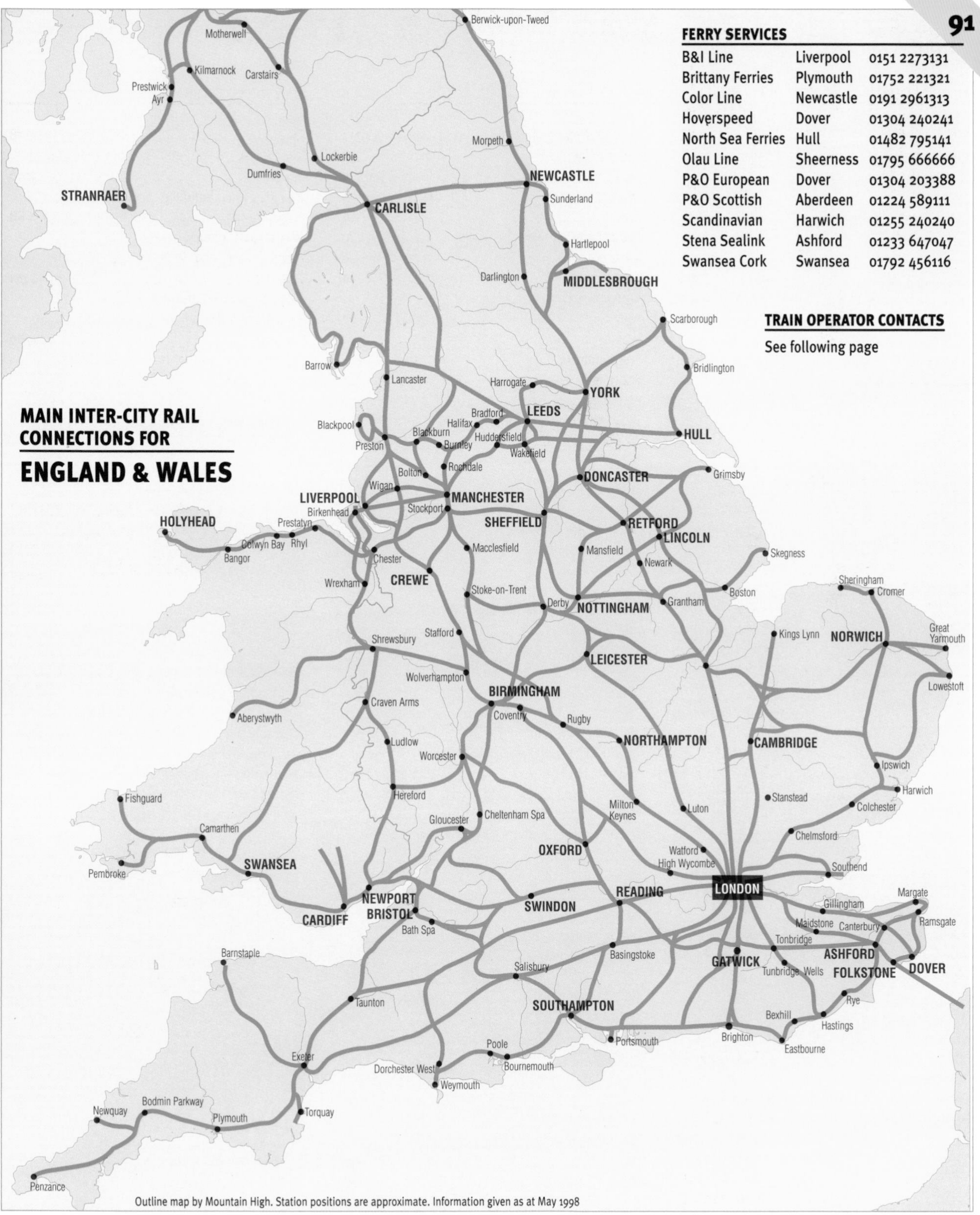

Outline map by Mountain High. Station positions are approximate. Information given as at May 1998

SUPPORTERS' AWAY INFORMATION

TRAIN OPERATORS

ANGLIA RAILWAYS
15-25 Artillery Lane, London, E1 7HA
Tel 01473 693333
Fax 01473 693497

CARDIFF RAILWAY CO
10th Floor, Brunel House, 2 Fitzalan Rd, Cardiff CF2 1SA
Tel 01222 430000
Fax 01222 480463

CENTRAL TRAINS
PO Box 4323, Stanier House, 10 Holliday Street Birmingham B1 1TH
Tel 0121 654 4444
Fax 0121 654 4461

CHILTERN RAILWAY CO
Western House, 14 Rickfords Hill, Aylesbury HP20 2RX
Tel 01296 332100
Fax 01296 332126

CONNEX SOUTH CENTRAL
Stephenson House, 2 Cherry Orchard Road, Croydon CR9 6JB
Tel 0181 667 2780
Fax 0181 667 2906

EUROSTAR (UK)
Eurostar House, Waterloo Station, London SE1 8SE
Tel 0171 928 5151

GATWICK EXPRESS
52 Grosvenor Gardens, London SW1W OAU
Tel 0171 973 5005
Fax 0171 973 5038

GREAT EASTERN RAILWAY
Hamilton House, 3 Appold Street, London EC2A 2AA
Tel 0645 50 50 00
Fax 01473 693745

GREAT NORTH EATERN RAILWAY
Main Headquarters Building, York YO1 1HT
Tel 01904 653022
Fax 01904 523392

GREAT WESTERN TRAINS CO
Milford House, 1 Milton Street, Swindon SN1 1HL
Tel 01793 499400
Fax 01793 499460

HEATHROW EXPRESS
4th Floor, Cardinal Point, Newall Rd, Hounslow Middlesex TW6 2QS
Tel 0181 745 0578
Fax 0181 745 1627

ISLAND LINE
Ryde St Johns Road Station, Ryde, Isle Of Wight PO33 2BA
Tel 01983 812591
Fax 01983 817879

LTS RAIL
Central House, Clifftown Road, Southend-on-Sea SS1 1AB
Tel 01702 357889

MERSEYRAIL ELECTRICS
Rail House, Lord Nelson Street, Liverpool L1 1JF
Tel 0151 709 8292
Fax 0151 702 2413

MIDLAND MAINLINE
Midland House, Nelson Street, Derby, East Midlands DE1 2SA
Tel 0345 221125
Fax 01332 262011

NORTH WESTERN TRAINS
PO Box 44, Rail House, Store Street Manchester M60 1DQ
Tel 0161 228 2141
Fax 0161 228 5003

REGIONAL RAILWAYS NORTH EAST
Main Headquarters Building, York YO1 1HT
Tel 01904 653022

SCOTRAIL RAILWAYS
Caledonian Chambers, 87 Union Street Glasgow G1 3TA
Tel 0141 332 9811

SILVERLINK TRAIN SERVICES
65-67 Clarendon Raod, Watford WD1 1DP
Tel 01923 207258
Fax 01923 207023

SOUTH WEST TRAINS
Friars Bridge Court, 41-45 Blackfrairs Road London SE1 8NZ
Tel 0171 928 5151
Fax 0171 902 3208

THAMESLINK RAIL
Friars Bridge, 41-45 Blackfriars Road, London SE1 8NZ
Tel 0171 620 5760
Fax 0171 620 5099

THAMES TRAINS
Venture House, 37 Blagrave Street, Reading RG1 1PZ
Tel 0118 908 3678
Fax 0118 957 9006

VIRGIN TRAINS
85 Smallbrook Queensway, Birmingham B5 4HA
Tel 0121 654 7400
Fax 0121 654 7487

WALES & WEST
Brunel House, 2 Fitzalan Rd, Cardiff CF2 1SU
Tel 01222 430400
Fax 01222 430214

WEST ANGLIA GREAT NORTHERN RAILWAY
Hertford House, 1 Cranwood Street, London EC1V 9GT
Tel 0345 818919
Fax 01223 453606

WEST COAST RAILWAY COMPANY
Warton Road, Carnforth, Lancashire LA5 9HX
Tel 01524 732100
Fax 01524 735518

SOCCER RELATED INTERNET BOOKMARKS

The following three pages are a listing of soccer websites, some of which you may find useful to bookmark. As any internet browser will know all too well, URLs change, move or become obsolete at the drop of a hat. At the time of going to press all the ones listed were active.

If you are new to internet browsing, the following information on entering the URL addresses should be observed. Because of the way the address lines are printed, those longer than the width of the column are broken into two lines, the second slightly indented. Nevertheless, all the characters of the address should be typed in as one line, with no spaces between characters. If your edition or version of browser already enters the 'http://' characters, or does not require them, omit these from the URL address.

Where sites are official, it states so in brackets after the site name. Any useful notes about the site are given after the name in square brackets.

WORLD CUP RELATED PAGES

Football Web in Japan
http://www.nidnet.com/link/socweb.html
CBS SportsLine - Soccer
http://www.sportsline.com/u/soccer/index.html
Teams of the World
http://www.islandia.is/totw/
World Cup - Soccernet
http://www.soccernet.com/u/soccer/worldcup98/index.html
World Cup 1998 - CBS SportsLine
http://www.sportsline.com/u/soccer/worldcup98/qualifying/index.html
World Cup Soccer - France 98 - Coupe du Monde
http://www.worldcup.com/english/index.html

FOOTBALL RELATED

1997 edition of the Laws of the Game
http://www.fifa.com/fifa/handbook/laws/index.laws.html
Soccer Books [good reference]
http://www.soccer-books.co.uk
British Society of Sports History [reference material]
http://www.umist.ac.uk/UMIST_Sport/bssh.html
Buchanan Brigade Messge Bd Thirty-Three
http://www.buchanan.org/mb33.html
Communicata Football
http://www.communicata.co.uk/lookover/football/
Division 1 Web Pages [relates to the Nationwide leagues]
http://www.users.globalnet.co.uk/~emmas/ndiv1.htm
Division 2 Web Pages [old Endsleigh rather than the Nationwide]
http://www.uwm.edu/People/dyce/htfc/clubs/div2-www.html
England [Engerland]
http://www.users.dircon.co.uk/~england/england/
England [Green Flags England team pages]
http://www.greenflag.co.uk/te/fslist.html
England [English Soccernet - National Team - News]
http://www.soccernet.com/english/national/news/index.html
England
http://www.englandfc.com/
English Club Homepages
http://pluto.webbernet.net/~bob/engclub.html
FAI - Irish International
http://www.fai.ie/
GeordieSport!
http://www.geordiepride.demon.co.uk/geordiesport.htm
L & M Referees' Society - Soccer Pages
http://www.lancs.ac.uk/ug/williams/soccer.htm
Northern Ireland [Norn Iron!: The NI International Football 'zine]
http://students.un.umist.ac.uk/gbh/index.html
Notts Association
http://www.innotts.co.uk/~soccerstats/gallery/nmf8.htm
Scotland [Rampant Scotland - Sport]
http://scotland.rampant.com/sport.htm
Scotland
http://web.city.ac.uk/~sh393/euro/scotland.htm
Scottish Football Association (Official)
http://www.scottishfa.co.uk/
Scottish Mailing Lists
http://www.isfa.com/isfa/lists/scotland.htm
Simply the Best
http://www.int-foot-fame.com/famers1.htm
Soccer ScoreSheet History List
http://www.kazmax.demon.co.uk/websheet/tm000309.htm
Soccer-Tables
http://www.marwin.ch/sport/fb/index.e.html
SoccerSearch: Players:G-P
http://www.soccersearch.com/Players/G-P/
SoccerSpace, Football & Soccer Links
http://www.winbet.sci.fi/soccerspace/links.htm
Team England - Fixtures & Results
http://ourworld.compuserve.com/homepages/nic_king/england/fixtures.htm
The Association of Football Statisticians
http://www.innotts.co.uk/~soccerstats/
The Aylesbury Branch of the Referees Association
http://homepages.bucks.net/~bigmick/
The Daily Soccer
http://www.dailysoccer.com/
The Football Supporters' Association (FSA)
http://www.fsa.org.uk/
US Soccer History Archives
http://www.sover.net/~spectrum/index.html
Welsh Football,Football wales,faw,welsh fa,ryan giggs
http://www.citypages.co.uk/faw/

ENGLISH PREMIERSHIP

Arsenal
http://www.arsenal.co.uk/
Aston Villa
http://www.geocities.com/Colosseum/Field/6089/
Aston Villa
http://www.villan.demon.co.uk/
Aston Villa
http://www.gbar.dtu.dk/~c937079/AVFC/index.html
Aston Villa (Official)
http://www.gbar.dtu.dk/~c937079/CB/
Barnsley
http://www.geocities.com/Colosseum/Field/6059/bfc.html
Barnsley
http://www.u-net.com/westex/bfc.htm
Barnsley
http://www.radders.skynet.co.uk/
Barnsley
http://upload.virgin.net/d.penty/Copacabarnsley/Copacabarnsley.htm
Barnsley
http://members.aol.com/JLister/bfc/bfc.htm
Blackburn Rovers
http://www.brfc-supporters.org.uk/
Blackburn Rovers (Official)
http://www.rovers.co.uk/
Bolton Wanderers
http://www.hankins.demon.co.uk/bwscl/index.html
Bolton Wanderers
http://www.netcomuk.co.uk/~cjw/football.html
Bolton Wanderers
http://www.geocities.com/Colosseum/4433/
Bolton Wanderers
http://mail.freeway.co.uk/druid/
Bolton Wanderers (Official)
http://www.boltonwfc.co.uk/
Charlton Athletic
http://www.demon.co.uk/casc/index.html
Chelsea
http://www.geocities.com/Colosseum/1457/chelsea.html
Chelsea
http://web.ukonline.co.uk/Members/jf.lettice/cfcmain.html
Chelsea
http://www.jack.dircon.net/chelsea/
Chelsea
http://fans-of.chelsea-fc.com/csr/
Chelsea FC (Official)
http://www.chelseafc.co.uk/chelsea/frontpage.shtml
Coventry City [mpegs of goals... that's it]
http://karpaty.tor.soliton.com/ccfcgoals/
Coventry City [The Sky Blue Superplex]
http://www.geocities.com/TimesSquare/Dungeon/1641/page4.html
Coventry City
http://www.warwick.ac.uk/~cudbu/SkyBlues.html
Coventry City (Official)
http://www.ccfc.co.uk/
Derby County
http://lard.sel.cam.ac.uk/derby_county/
Derby County
http://www.cheme.cornell.edu/~jwillits/this.html
Derby County
http://easyweb.easynet.co.uk/~nickwheat/ramsnet.html
Derby County
http://home.sol.no/~einasand/derby.htm
Derby County
http://www.cheme.cornell.edu/~jwillits/derby2.html#History
Derby County
http://www.derby-county.com/main.htm
Derby County (Official)
http://www.dcfc.co.uk/dcfc/index.html
Everton FC (Official)
http://www.connect.org.uk/everton/
Leeds United
http://www.lufc.co.uk/
Leeds United
http://spectrum.tcns.co.uk/cedar/leeds.htm
Leeds United
http://www.csc.liv.ac.uk/users/tim/Leeds/
Leeds United (Official - CarlingNet)
http://www.fa-premier.com/club/lufc/
Leicester City (Official)
http://www.lcfc.co.uk/141097b.htm
Liverpool
http://akureyri.ismennt.is/~jongeir/
Liverpool
http://www.soccernet.com/livrpool/
Liverpool
http://www.connect.org.uk/anfield/
Manchester United
http://www.cs.indiana.edu/hyplan/ccheah/posts.html
Manchester United
http://www.geocities.com/SouthBeach/6367/index.html
Manchester United
http://www.sky.co.uk/sports/manu/
Manchester United
http://www.cybernet.dk/users/barrystorv/
Manchester United
http://home.pacific.net.sg/~jerping/
Manchester United
http://sunhehi.phy.uic.edu/~clive/MUFC/home.html
Manchester United
http://www.iol.ie/~mmurphy/red_devils/mufc.htm
Manchester United
http://www.davewest.demon.co.uk/
Manchester United
http://www.webcom.com/~solution/mufc/manu.html
Manchester United
http://ourworld.compuserve.com/homepages/red_devil/
Manchester United
http://xanadu.centrum.is/~runarhi/
Manchester United
http://web.city.ac.uk/~sh393/mufc.htm
Manchester United
http://www.wsu.edu:8080/~mmarks/Giggs.html
Manchester United
http://osiris.sunderland.ac.uk/online/access/manutd/redshome.html
Manchester United
http://www.u-net.com/~pitman/
Manchester United
http://www.geocities.com/Colosseum/2483/
Manchester United
http://www.wsu.edu:8080/~mmarks/mufclinks.html
Manchester United
http://gladstone.uoregon.edu:80/~jsetzen/mufc.html
Manchester United
http://members.hknet.com/~siukin/
Newcastle United
http://www.swan.co.uk/TOTT
Newcastle United
http://www.nufc.com
Newcastle United
http://www.btinternet.com/~the.magpie/history1.htm
Newcastle United
http://www.ccacyber.com/nufc/
Newcastle United
http://sunflower.singnet.com.sg/~resa21/
Nottingham Forest
http://users.homenet.ie/~aidanhut/
Nottingham Forest
http://www.thrustworld.co.uk/users/kryten/forest/
Nottingham Forest
http://hem1.passagen.se/pearce/index.htm
Nottingham Forest
http://www.innotts.co.uk/~joe90/forest.htm
Nottingham Forest
http://ourworld.compuserve.com/homepages/kencrossland/
Nottingham Forest (Official)
http://www.nottingham-forest.co.uk/frames.html
Sheffield Wednesday
http://www.crg.cs.nott.ac.uk/Users/anb/Football/stats/swfcarch.htm
Sheffield Wednesday
http://www.rhi.hi.is/~jbj/sheffwed/opnun.htm

BOOKMARKS

Sheffield Wednesday
http://www.geocities.com/Colosseum/2938/
Sheffield Wednesday
http://www.cs.nott.ac.uk/~anb/Football/
Southampton [Saintsweb]
http://www.soton.ac.uk/~saints/
Southampton [Marching In]
http://www.saintsfans.com/marchingin/
Tottenham Hotspur [White Hart Site]
http://www.xpress.se/~ssab0019/webring/index.html
Tottenham Hotspur [Felix Gills' Page]
http://www.gilnet.demon.co.uk/spurs.htm
Tottenham Hotspur
http://www.personal.u-net.com/~spurs/
Tottenham Hotspur [check Spurs results year-by-year - just stats]
http://www.bobexcell.demon.co.uk/
Tottenham Hotspur
http://www.btinternet.com/~matt.cook/
Tottenham Hotspur (Official)
http://www.spurs.co.uk/welcome.html
West Ham United
http://www.ecs.soton.ac.uk/saints/premier/westham.htm
West Ham United
http://www.westhamunited.co.uk/
Wimbledon
http://www.fa-premier.com/cgi-bin/fetch/club/wfc/home.html?team='WIM'
Wimbledon [unofficial - WISA]
http://www.wisa.org.uk/
Wimbledon [Womble.Net - Independent Wimbledon FC Internet 'zine]
http://www.geocities.com/SunsetStrip/Studio/6112/womblnet.html
Wimbledon [very basic]
http://www.aracnet.com/~davej/football.htm
Wimbledon [unofficial - USA]
http://soyokaze.biosci.ohio-state.edu/~dcp/wimbledon/womble.html
Wimbledon
http://www.city.ac.uk/~sh393/prem/wimbeldon.htm
Wimbledon
http://www.netkonect.co.uk/b/brenford/wimbledon/
Wimbledon [unofficial - WISA]
http://www.soi.city.ac.uk/homes/ec564/donswisa.html
Wimbledon [John's Wimbledon FC page]
http://www.soi.city.ac.uk/homes/ec564/dons.top.html
Wimbledon (Official)
http://www.wimbledon-fc.co.uk/

ENGLISH DIVISION 1

Birmingham City [PlanetBlues]
http://www.isfa.com/server/web/planetblues/
Birmingham City [BCFC Supports Club Redditch Branch]
http://www.fortunecity.com/olympia/ovett/135/
Birmingham City [Richy's B'ham City Page]
http://www.rshill.demon.co.uk/blues.htm
Bradford City
http://www.legend.co.uk/citygent/index.html
Bury
http://www.brad.ac.uk/%7edjmartin/bury1.html
Crystal Palace
http://www.gold.net/users/az21/cp_home.htm
Fulham [The Independent Fulham Fans Website: History]
http://www.fulhamfc.co.uk/History/history.html
Fulham [FulhamWeb]
http://www.btinternet.com/~aredfern/
Fulham [Black & White Pages]
http://www.wilf.demon.co.uk/fulhamfc/ffc.html
Fulham [unofficial - The Fulham Football Club Mailing List]
http://www.users.dircon.co.uk/~troyj/fulham/
Fulham
http://zeus.bris.ac.uk/~chmsl/fulham/fulham.html
Fulham
http://www.netlondon.com/cgi-local/wilma/spo.873399737.html
Fulham (Official) [mostly merchandising]
http://www.fulham-fc.co.uk/
Huddersfield Town
http://www.geocities.com/Colosseum/4401/index.html
Huddersfield Town
http://ftp.csd.uwm.edu/People/dyce/htfc/
Huddersfield Town
http://granby.nott.ac.uk/~ppykara/htfc/
Huddersfield Town
http://www.uwm.edu:80/~dyce/htfc/index.html
Ipswich Town [MATCHfacts - Datafile]
http://www.matchfacts.com/mfdclub/ipswich.htm
Ipswich Town
http://www.sys.uea.ac.uk/Recreation/Sport/itfc/
Ipswich Town [Those Were The Days]
http://www.twtd.co.uk/
Ipswich Town
http://members.wbs.net/homepages/a/d/a/adamcable.html
Ipswich Town [The Online Portman Vista]
http://www.btinternet.com/~bluearmy/index2.html
Ipswich Town [unofficial - Latest News - not really]
http://www.rangey.demon.co.uk/ipswich.htm
Ipswich Town [IPSWICH TOWN tribute]
http://www.geocities.com/Colosseum/Track/5399/
Ipswich Town [The Ipswich Town VRML Site - techy, not much else]
http://www.sys.uea.ac.uk/Recreation/Sport/itfc/vrml/vrml.html
Ipswich Town
http://homepages.enterprise.net/meo/itfc2.html
Ipswich Town (Official)
http://www.itfc.co.uk/
Manchester City
http://www.uit.no/mancity/
Manchester City (Official)
http://www.mcfc.co.uk/
Middlesbrough
http://www.hk.super.net/~tlloyd/personal/boro.html
Norwich City
http://ncfc.netcom.co.uk/ncfc/
Oxford United
http://www.aligrafix.co.uk/ag/fun/home/OxTales/default.html
Oxford United
http://www.netlink.co.uk//users/oufc1/index.html
Port Vale
http://www.netcentral.co.uk/~iglover/index.html
Port Vale
http://web.dcs.hull.ac.uk/people/pjp/PortVale/PortVale.html
Portsmouth [unofficial - History]
http://www.mech.port.ac.uk/StaffP/pb/history.html
Portsmouth [Links page]
http://www.imsport.co.uk/imsport/ims/tt/035/club.html
Queens Park Rangers
http://www-dept.cs.ucl.ac.uk/students/M.Pemble/index.html
Reading
http://www.i-way.co.uk/~readingfc/
Sheffield United
http://www.shef.ac.uk/city/blades/
Sheffield United
http://pine.shu.ac.uk/~cmssa/bifa.html
Sheffield United (Official)
http://www.sufc.co.uk/
Stoke City
http://www.cs.bham.ac.uk/~jdr/scfc/scfc.htm
Sunderland (Official)
http://www.sunderland-afc.com/
Swindon Town
http://www.bath.ac.uk/~ee3cmk/swindon/home.html
Tranmere Rovers
http://www.connect.org.uk/merseyworld/tarantula/
Tranmere Rovers
http://www.brad.ac.uk/~mjhesp/tran.htm
West Bromwich Albion
http://pages.prodigy.com/FL/baggie/
West Bromwich Albion
http://www.gold.net/users/cp78/
West Bromwich Albion - Official
http://www.wba.co.uk/
Wolverhampton Wanderers [The Wandering Wolf]
http://www.angelfire.com/wv/Quants/index.html
Wolverhampton Wanderers
http://www.lazy-dog.demon.co.uk/wolves/
Wolverhampton Wanderers (Official)
http://www.idiscover.co.uk/wolves/

ENGLISH DIVISION 2

AFC Bournemouth
http://www.bath.ac.uk/~ee6dlah/club.htm
AFC Bournemouth
http://www.homeusers.prestel.co.uk/rose220/afcb1.htm
AFC Bournemouth
http://www.maths.soton.ac.uk/rpb/AFCB.html
AFC Bournemouth
http://www.maths.soton.ac.uk/rpb/AFCB.html
AFC Bournemouth
http://www.geocities.com/TimesSquare/Arcade/7499/afcb.htm
AFC Bournemouth (Official)
http://www.afcb.co.uk/
Blackpool
http://web.ukonline.co.uk/Members/c.moffat/basil/
Bristol City
http://ourworld.compuserve.com/homepages/redrobins/
Bristol Rovers
http://dialspace.dial.pipex.com/town/street/xko88/
Bristol Rovers
http://members.wbs.net/homepages/l/a/r/lardon/
Bristol Rovers
http://www.cf.ac.uk/uwcc/engin/brittonr/rovers/index.html
Bristol Rovers
http://www.geocities.com/Colosseum/6542/
Bristol Rovers
http://www.personal.unet.com/~coley/rovers/
Bristol Rovers
http://www.btinternet.com/~uk/BRFC/
Bristol Rovers
http://www.btinternet.com/~uk/BristolRovers/index.html
Bristol Rovers
http://www.cowan.edu.au/~gprewett/gas.htm
Bristol Rovers
http://www.cf.ac.uk/uwcc/engin/brittonr/rovers/index.html
Burnley
http://www.zensys.co.uk/home/page/trevor.ent/
Burnley
http://www.theturf.demon.co.uk/burnley.htm
Burnley
http://www.zen.co.uk/home/page/p.bassek/
Burnley
http://www.mtattersall.demon.co.uk/index.html
Burnley
http://home.sol.no/~parald/burnley/
Burnley
http://www.geocities.com/Colosseum/7075/index.html
Carlisle United
http://www.aston.ac.uk/~jonespm/
Carlisle United
http://dspace.dial.pipex.com/town/square/ad969/
Chester City [Silly Sausage - good history]
http://www.sillysausage.demon.co.uk/history.htm
Chester City (Official)
http://www.chester-city.co.uk/
Gillingham
http://ourworld.compuserve.com/homepages/gillsf.c/
Grimsby Town
http://www.aston.ac.uk/~etherina/index.html
Preston North End [unofficial - PNEWeb HomePage]
http://freespace.virgin.net/paul.billington/PNEWeb_homepage.html
Preston North End [unofficial - PNE Pages]
http://www.dpne.demon.co.uk/pages/pagesf.html
Preston North End [pie muncher online - front door]
http://www.pylonvu.demon.co.uk/pm/pm.html